Reading and Interpreting the Works of

AMY TAN

Enslow Publishing
101 W. 23rd Street
Suite 240
New York, NY 10011
USA
enslow.com

Lit Crit Guides

Reading and Interpreting the Works of

AMY TAN

Audrey Borus

Published in 2017 by Enslow Publishing, LLC
101 W. 23rd Street, Suite 240, New York, NY 10011

Library of Congress Cataloging-in-Publication Data
Names: Borus, Audrey, author.
Title: Reading and interpreting the works of Amy Tan / Audrey Borus.
Description: New York : Enslow Publishing, 2017. | Series: Lit crit guides |Includes bibliographical references and index.
Identifiers: LCCN 2015050605 | ISBN 9780766079168 (library bound)
Subjects: LCSH: Tan, Amy—Criticism and interpretation—Juvenile literature.
Classification: LCC PS3570.A48 Z58 2016 | DDC 813/.54—dc23
LC record available at http://lccn.loc.gov/2015050605

Printed in the United States of America

To Our Readers: We have done our best to make sure all website addresses in this book were active and appropriate when we went to press. However, the author and the publisher have no control over and assume no liability for the material available on those websites or on any websites they may link to. Any comments or suggestions can be sent by e-mail to customerservice@enslow.com.

Photo Credits: Cover, p. 3 Steve Sands/WireImage/Getty Images; vectorgraphics/Shutterstock.com (series logo); p. 6 Mark Mainz/Getty Images for AFI; p. 10 Culture Club/Hulton Archive/Getty Images; p. 17 Jeff Goode/Getty Images; p. 19 Ron Bull/Toronto Star/Getty Images; p. 24 Ron Galella Ltd./Ron Galella Collection/Getty Images; pp. 29, 33 Everett Collection; p. 40 Buena Vista/courtesy Everett Collection; p. 45 Megan Quick; p. 47 PHAS/UIG/Getty Images; p. 52 General Photographic Agency/Hulton Archive/Getty Images; p. 57 B. Anthony Stewart/National Geographic/Getty Images; p. 64 New York Daily News Archive/Getty Images; p. 67 EQRoy/Shutterstock.com; p. 70 DEA/L. DeMasi/De Agostini/Getty Images; p. 79 Peter Charlesworth/LightRocket/Getty Images; p. 80 Jay Directo/AFP/Getty Images; p. 84 Mireya Acierto/Getty Images; p. 87 Thos Robinson/WireImage/Getty Images; p. 89 Nancy Kaszeman/ZUMA Press.

Contents

Amy Tan

Coming to Gold Mountain

As a seven-year-old, Amy Tan remembers reading a book with her father, a collection of 365 stories. "The stories were supposed to be read in sequence, a story a day beginning with a sledding caper on a snowy January 1."[1] Tan recounts that as the year wore on she was able to read these stories herself and began to realize not very much happened in the lives of these children, a thing she found reassuring since her own life felt tumultuous enough. From the new homes to which the family was constantly moving, to the friend of hers who died and at whose funeral her mother whispered, "This what happen you don't listen to mother." Tan recalls herself as a "worrisome" child.[2]

The only daughter of Daisy (Du Ching) and John Tan, Amy Tan was born in Oakland, California, in 1952. Both her parents had emigrated from China only a few years before. During World War II, John Tan—whose language skills in Cantonese, Mandarin, and English were excellent—had worked for the American government and in 1947 came to the United States. He was an electrical engineer in Beijing and was offered a scholarship to the Massachusetts Institute of Technology (MIT) to further his studies. However, he gave up the scholarship and joined the ministry in Berkeley, California.

Daisy Tan arrived two years later. The two had met while John Tan was still in China and had started an affair, though

Coming to America

In the 1840s, most Chinese immigrants were from South China (Cantonese), and they came looking for gold. In fact, so many Chinese were coming to California, it became known as Gum San, or Gold Mountain. The immigrants of the 1840s and 50s were mainly men. They could not bring their wives or have families, nor could they become American citizens because of the Chinese Exclusion Act.

By the year 1940, things were different. China and the United States found themselves fighting together as allies against Japan, and China was in the midst of a civil war. The Chinese Exclusion Act was repealed, but there was still much prejudice. Says historian John Kuo Wei Tchen: "Leaving China you really didn't necessarily know if you are [sic] going to be able to gain access to the United States. You had to go to this detention center at Angel Island, which is in San Francisco Harbor next to Alcatraz."[3]

It's important to note that Angel Island was actually designed to keep immigrants out of the United States. There were rigorous examinations—physical and mental—which could last from less than an hour to several days and could include hundreds of questions. "The interrogation could be so difficult that applicants might rehearse for months in China, even when their claim to citizenship was perfectly valid."[4] And if they stumbled in any way, which given the stakes is understandable, they were not allowed entry into the United States.

As immigration laws became less overtly racist, more and more people came into the United States, bringing with them their culture. Immigrants began to feel comfortable speaking Chinese and different dialects. Tan's family was part of a group that builds up Oakland's and San Francisco's Chinatowns. They were not Cantonese, and they spoke Potunghua, a Mandarin dialect.[5]

Daisy had been married to an abusive army pilot at the time. For the affair, Daisy was briefly imprisoned. John Tan left for the United States. When she was released from prison, Daisy cabled John that she had finally obtained a divorce and that China would soon be taken over by the Communists. Should she come? John Tan said yes.

California, 1953

In some ways, 1950s California was the epitome of the American Dream. Newly discharged veterans of World War II, with money from the GI bill, were purchasing homes (at a fraction of their cost today) and cars. The gasoline to fuel these cars was plentiful, a material called "plastic" was invented, and manufacturing jobs were there for the taking. However, not everything was rosy.

Despite their independence during wartime, fewer women worked outside the home after the war was over because it was frowned upon. When they did work, their salary was often much less than their male counterparts. In the aftermath of the Korean War (1950–1953), feelings in the United States towards Asians were not always positive. US immigration laws still kept Asians out of the country. Those immigration laws were not changed until 1965. Tan's parents were able to emigrate because Tan's engineer father had skills that the United States needed at that time, but there were not nearly the number of Asians nationwide as there are today; Amy Tan reports she didn't feel "typical," and that her father being a Baptist minister made her even more "unusual."[6] She tried to make herself look more "American" by pinning a clothespin to her "too Chinese" nose. "Like a lot of Chinese-American children, I grew up with a lot of self-hate."[7]

This illustration depicts a Chinese neighborhood in San Francisco in the late 1800s. Many Chinese immigrants, Tan's family included, continued to make their homes in California well into the twentieth century.

Home and Education

John Tan grew up in a religious household. His father was Presbyterian, converted by missionaries in Canton and educated in their English language schools. In fact, every one of the twelve Tan children became a preacher or minister. Tan's mother, Daisy, on the other hand, believed more in the Chinese notion of fate.

Though Daisy had been abused by her former husband in China, she was still not able to obtain custody of her three children because Chinese law at the time did not allow a divorcée to keep them. Tan's mother kept them a secret from her new family. [8]

The Tans moved a lot during Amy's childhood. She writes: "Every six to twelve months we had to move to another house. Whenever my mother became unhappy, she wanted to leave. And once she locked on to an idea, she could not let it go, until her unhappiness permeated the entire house and she made us ill with her nonstop complaints. By the time I graduated from high school I had attended 11 schools."[9]

As an adult, Tan reflects that the constant moving was good training for a writer, as she had to learn to adjust and observe. "It sharpened my skills of observation. It deepened my sense of alienation, which while not a prerequisite for a writer, is certainly useful as an impetus for writing."[10]

Tan had a tumultuous relationship with her mother. She jokes that the consequences of not minding her were dire. While other people's parents might caution their children to look both ways when crossing the street, her mother's version was, "You don't look, you get smash flat like sand dab."[11] Her mother was also ruled by old-world superstition and magical thinking; for example, she believed in ghosts and thought her

THE ULTIMATE AMERICAN SYMBOL: ROUTE 66

When Amy Tan was born, America had survived the Great Depression and World War II. There was great optimism in the United States as the economy began to boom. Young men who had returned from the war were starting families and buying houses. Many decided to move to the West Coast, where the American Dream seemed to be there for the taking. One of the major routes for those traveling west was Route 66. "No single artifact of popular culture embraced the post-war Route 66 adventure so richly as did the hit song by which most people probably still know its lore and legend, Bobby Troup's 'Get Your Kicks on Route 66.'"[12]

daughter had a talent for seeing them. According to Tan, her "morbid imagination" is due to the fact that her mother so often talked about death and dying.[13]

When Amy was fifteen, her father and elder brother died of brain tumors within months of one another. Her mother, who had previously embraced God, stopped praying. Daisy Tan hired a geomancer (a person who tells the future by geographic features, figures, or lines) to rid their home of evil spirits, and she decided that moving abroad was the only way to avoid further bad luck. For three years she, her mother, and brother moved continuously. The three settled down, first in Holland, and then in Montreux, Switzerland, where Tan completed high school. While in Montreux, her classmates were the children of ambassadors, wealthy businessmen, and nobility. But what Tan remembers most is that she found her first boyfriend, "a frizzy-haired hippie whose father had been a Nazi officer."[14] The boyfriend, named Franz, told Tan he had deserted from the German army; he turned out to be a psychiatric patient who wanted her to elope with him. Tan's mother got wind of the situation. The police were alerted, found drugs, and arrested Franz and his friends. Tan was released while the others were jailed and deported. Shortly after, Tan finished high school and returned to the United States to attend college in Oregon.

From an early age, Tan says that there were expectations that she would become a doctor. Once in college, Amy Tan became interested in English literature and majored in English and linguistics, much to her mother's disappointment. After transferring to San Jose City College and then to San Jose State, Tan received her bachelor's degree. She then went to UC (Santa Cruz and then Berkeley) for postgraduate work in linguistics but dropped out.

During college and after, Tan held an assortment of jobs: switchboard operator, carhop for A&W fast-food restaurant, bartender, and pizza maker at The Round Table (another fast-food franchise). Eventually, she became a consultant to the Alameda County Association for Retarded Citizens and helped developmentally disabled children. As one of a few Asian Americans in the job, she found she was thrust into the position of minority expert. Interestingly, this is a recurring theme for Tan—she is often pigeonholed as an Asian-American writer, a label she does not like because she feels her writing is about much more than "minority" issues.

Uncomfortable in her role in Alameda, Tan decided to try her skills as a writer. Initially she teamed up with a friend who ran a medical publishing business, and then struck out on her own as a freelance business writer. Quickly she became successful, working on projects for AT&T, IBM, and Bank of America, and as word got out about her skills as a business

Making the Mainstream

Before *The Joy Luck Club* was published, two of the stories appeared in a modified format in popular magazines. "The Rules of the Game" appeared in *Seventeen* magazine in 1986, and the title story, "The Joy Luck Club," appeared in *Ladies' Home Journal* in 1989. According to critic Matthew James Vechinski, both magazines removed details from the stories, which has the effect of simplifying the "stories' representation of Chinese-American families and peer groups."[15] This, in turn, dilutes an important theme in Tan's work: what it means to be between two cultures. It also forces a much more shallow reading of Tan's work. "The longer book version of 'The Rules of the Game' suggests that Waverly's success at chess forces her into maturity while she is still a child," but the details about Waverly losing her youth are removed from the *Seventeen* version.[16] In the *Ladies' Home Journal* version of "The Joy Luck Club," there is no mention of the fact that June has been evicted from her apartment, as one of the mothers (Auntie Ying) boasts that her daughter Lena is buying an expensive apartment in a great neighborhood.

Ultimately, Vechinski suggests that these popular magazines are more concerned about "connecting with their female audiences,"[17] than with the larger issues of identity across cultures, but it is interesting to note that editors at both magazines cut material that anchors the characters as very distinct products of their heritage, thus rendering them flat. Further, the myriad and complex issues Tan touches upon in her novel are reduced to a rather one-dimensional theme about mother-daughter relationships.

writer, there was more demand for her services. She found she wasn't able to turn away work and was at one point clocking ninety hours a week.[18] Busy though she was, this type of writing was unfulfilling. Tan came up with a plan to beat the boredom: study jazz piano and take on only the assignments that interested her. She read a lot during this period as well.

It was during this time that Tan wrote her first short piece about a Chinese chess prodigy who has a difficult relationship with her mother. Called "Endgame," the story was published in *FM Magazine* and later in *Seventeen*. With the story written, she was able to attend a writer's workshop directed by the novelist Oakley Hall. At the workshop she met other writers, who gave her suggestions.

Encouraged, Tan tried writing another story. She heard from California-based literary agent Sandra Dijkstra, who had read "Endgame" and wanted to see more of Tan's work. Meanwhile, a friend called to congratulate Tan on her status as an international writer. Tan discovered that without her knowledge or consent, "Endgame" had been translated into Italian. Recalling the literary agent's inquiry, Tan asked whether Dijkstra would represent her. Dijkstra asked to see another story Tan was writing at the time, titled "Waiting Between the Trees." Dijkstra agreed to represent her, and the two began to explore whether Tan's work was a series of short stories or an actual novel.

2 Major Themes

To date, Amy Tan has written nine books of fiction and hundreds of articles and essays. She is probably best known for *The Joy Luck Club*. As Gayle Feldman noted in an article for *Publisher's Weekly*, Tan's debut novel won her almost instant fame and had all the makings of a publishing legend.[1]

Thanks to Tan's success in writing about the Asian American experience, many have looked to her as a spokeswoman for an entire group of people. She has said that she is "alarmed when reviewers and educators assume that my very personal, specific and fictional stories are meant to be representative, down to the smallest detail of not just Chinese-Americans but sometimes all Asian culture."[2] While it would be reductive to see her as only a mouthpiece for minority women writers, she *is* Asian American as much as she is a female, and her writing is in some ways informed by this. Literary scholar E. D. Huntley suggests that Tan's fiction is "ethnic in the sense that it is the product of the imagination of an author who is a second-generation Chinese American, a writer who is interested in and well-informed about the cultural, geographical and historical borders of her life and that of her immigrant parents." By giving a voice to that community, Tan speaks for and to it, "reflecting its traditions and cultural structures, and articulating its values and concerns."[3]

"Writing is an extreme privilege but it's also a gift," says Tan. "It's a gift to yourself and it's a gift of giving a story to someone."

The style of Tan's major works such as *The Joy Luck Club*, *The Kitchen God's Wife*, and *The Hundred Secret Senses* seems more experimental than the traditional linear narrative, where one scene logically follows another. Rather, Tan's novels make use of myths, fables, poetry, dreams and visions—a "textual collage," says Huntley.[4] In this way Tan can explore important issues from the perspective of more than one character.

Many of Tan's works use the "talk story," a form of traditional oral Chinese storytelling that chronicles the drama of real-life family stories.[5] According to writer and critic Linda Ching Sledge, talk stories were never intended to be heard by non-Chinese listeners. They often contain Chinese parables and proverbs, along with old country wisdom.

Huntley suggests that Tan's characters use the talk-story because their "ties to Chinese tradition remain strong. In their attempts to explain their lives to their daughters the mothers in *The Joy Luck Club* and *The Kitchen God's Wife* . . . draw on traditional oral forms to shape their stories and to disguise the urgency and seriousness with which they are attempting to transmit to their daughters the remnants of a culture that is fading even from their own lives."[6] In other words, the older generation uses conversation and stories to impart to their children important traditions and values; for example, the idea

fable

A story intended to teach a lesson, in which animals take on the characteristics of humans.

myth

A story, often involving gods or other superhuman beings, that is told in order to explain a custom, belief, or event.

perspective

Point of view.

Amy Tan poses for a photo in 1990. While her works center around the Asian-American experience, she balks at the idea that her novels are representative of an entire culture.

that one is part of a community as opposed to the American ideal of individualism.

Another major theme in Tan's work is personal and group identity. Tan has said that her parents wanted her and her brothers to "think Chinese" but always speak perfect English. In essence, the Tans wanted their children to take advantage of their American circumstances and to be part of the American mainstream, but to somehow stand apart from it.[7] That balancing act is the stuff of Tan's novels. In speaking about *The Joy Luck Club* in particular, Tan has said, "I don't think I started to think about any of this until I started to write the book . . . I think what I was trying to find was how can you have the best of both worlds; how can you keep your Chinese face and keep your American face and not hide anything and not be dishonest. I think for me personally the book is a lot about finding balance."[8]

Food is another thematic convention Tan uses. In most cultures, food brings people together. In Amy Tan's novels, food is a way of joining people, but it is also a way of setting the time period. For example, in *The Kitchen God's Wife*, Tan details staples of the prewar Chinese kitchen: peanut oil, soy sauce, sticky rice cakes stuffed with date paste.[9] She takes great care to describe how a New Year's meal is prepared, emphasizing the sense of celebration and communalism required for its preparation. In Tan's novels, food is not only for sustenance; it brings people together.

In this book, we will examine three of Tan's novels: *The Joy Luck Club*, *The Kitchen God's Wife*, and *The Bonesetter's Daughter*. They provide excellent examples of each of the themes described here. Readers will also be introduced to Tan's recent work, *The Valley of Amazemen*t. Though something of a departure for Tan in that she writes about the life of courtesans (and therefore sex), it also explores her tried-and-true themes: mother/daughter relationships, the idea of self-identity, and the way different people respond to their circumstances.

The Joy Luck Club

Published in 1988, when Tan was just thirty-six years old, *The Joy Luck Club* was an immediate success. Before the year was over, the book was named as a selection for the Book-of-the Month Club and the Quality Paperback Club. *The Joy Luck Club* remained on the *New York Times* bestseller list for thirty-four weeks in hardcover, "flourished in paperback for nine months and abroad in twenty-five languages," won an American Library Association Best Book For Young Adults award, and was a finalist for the National Book Award.[1] Interestingly, it did not do well in China.

The novel centers around four Chinese mothers, who are the Joy Luck Club, and their American-born daughters. Composed of sixteen chapters, each a story in itself, the book chronicles the lives of the mother-daughter pairs: June (Jing-Mei Woo) and her mother, Suyuan Woo (who has recently died); An-Mei Hsu and her daughter Rose; Lindo Jong and her daughter Waverly, and Ying-Ying St. Clair and her daughter Lena.

When interviewed about the book's success, Tan suggested that it was the right book at the right time. Baby boomers were having children and were thinking about their relationships with their own mothers. "Sometimes I think it's because I'm a Baby-Boomer and what I wrote about are very normal emotions and conflicts that many people have, so somehow it struck a universal chord. I think that I was in the right time

Tan poses with a copy of her picture book, *The Moon Lady*, in 1992.

and the right place. I met the right people, who were passionate about my work and, thus, able to get it in front of people who would sell the book in bookstores, readers who would pass the word along to their mothers or daughters or friends. I think it's all of that."[2]

Plot

Throughout the book, each mother and daughter pair recall significant events in their lives that reveal who they are, the nature of their relationships, and the way they respond to their Chinese heritage. The novel develops bit by bit as each woman's story unfolds and intertwines. June, whose mother, Suyuan, has died just before the novel opens, is the first to narrate. According to E. D. Huntley, this is critical because it is through June more than any other narrator (with the exception of Rose), that we learn of the connections between this group of mothers and daughters; how their dreams and concerns intersect. June's narrative also sets the stage for the "issues on which the novel focuses: the struggle for control between mothers and daughters; the daughters' bids for independent lives; the mothers' attempts to understand the dynamics of life in the New World and somehow to blend the best of their Old World culture with a new way of life that they do not comprehend."[3]

As we are introduced to the charter members of the club, which started when the mothers were newly arrived from China, we learn that the club was a way for them to gather, compare notes on immigrant life, and play mah-jongg, a popular game in China, where four players sit around a table and strategically pick tiles. Their meetings are a time to eat familiar food, drink tea, gamble, and take a break from day-to-day worries. We also meet each of the club members'

American daughters. To fill the empty spot left by the recent death of founding member Suyuan, her daughter June joins the table. Aware that "circumstances have changed her interaction [with) her mother's peers—Chinese born immigrants and the mothers of [her] childhood friends, [June] revisits her memories of her mother and comes to see their relationship in a different light."[4]

By placing June at the table, Tan allows her to become the bridge between the conflicts of tradition versus the new, young verses old. It also helps the mothers realize that in some ways, their daughters are strangers.

Feathers From a Thousand Li Away

The novel opens with this passage:

> The old woman remembered a swan she had bought many years ago in Shanghai for a foolish sum. This bird, boasted the market vendor, was once a duck that stretched its neck in hopes of becoming a goose, and now look!—it is too beautiful to eat.
>
> Then the woman and the swan sailed across an ocean many thousands of li wide, stretching their necks toward America. On her journey she cooed to the swan: "In America I will have a daughter just like me. But over there nobody will say her worth is measured by the loudness of her husband's belch. Over there nobody will look down on her, because I will make her speak only perfect American English. And over there she will always be too full to swallow any sorrow! She will know my meaning, because I will give her this swan—a creature that became more than what was hoped for.[5]

This opening is important because it sets the tone for the entire novel, a balancing act between two seeming opposites:

ONE CRITIC'S VIEW

Tara Fickle, assistant professor of English and Asian literature at the University of Oregon, says that response to *The Joy Luck Club* has been divided along cultural lines. On the one hand, it was praised for exposing the reading public, which is largely white, to a demographic—Asians and Asian Americans—to which they might not be familiar. It was also praised for its ability to "foster a 'sister-centered' sense of community both within and beyond the text itself."[6] On the other hand, it is that very quality that literary critics point to when they criticize Tan's writing and particularly *The Joy Luck Club*. They believe that true literature should "disturb the mind and derange the senses,"[7] and is not meant to be easy or "feel-good." Sau-ling Cynthia Wong has been one of Tan's harshest critics, calling those who read and like Tan "a sugar-sisterhood."[8]

Professor Fickle points out that those who are particularly critical of Tan, like Wong, tend to be Asian American, and that one of their biggest complaints about *The Joy Luck Club* is that it isn't serious enough and that it "caters to rather than challenges stereotypical assumptions" about a certain ethnic group. That's ironic, Fickle notes, because in this type of objection, the critics are themselves engaging in a stereotype: "[T]hat appraisal seems paradoxical, if not downright counterproductive, when one recognizes that it . . . replicates one of the most basic stereotypes about Asian Americans: that their achievements as a model minority are the product of a near-ascetic eschewal [avoidance] of all things fun and an almost fanatical dedication to the serious pursuits of economic and scholastic success."[9]

East versus West, hope versus despair, traditional versus new-fangled.

In the first section, we are introduced to the club's members. There is Suyuan Woo, founder of the Joy Luck Club. Through June, we learn that Suyuan Woo escaped from Kweilin (a city in southern China) in advance of the Japanese invasion. Because circumstances were so dire, Suyuan was forced to abandon her two twin baby girls. At the first club gathering after Suyuan Woo's death, the Joy Luck Club aunties tell June that the twins are alive in China. Her mother had searched for them for years and had finally traced them to an address to which the aunties have written. They have taken a collection of their mah-jongg winnings and present it to June, with the suggestion that she go to China to visit her half-sisters and celebrate her mother's life.

Next we hear from An-Mei Hsu. She relates how her mother leaves the family to become a concubine of Wu Tsing, a rich merchant, while she is brought up by her grandmother, Popo. (A concubine is a woman who lives with a man but does not have the status of wife.) Popo refuses to discuss An-Mei's mother, but when Popo becomes sick, An-Mei's mother returns to care for her. Popo dies and An-Mei goes with her mother to live in the merchant's home. Gradually, she learns that her mother was forced to marry this man and had a son by him, but that the son has been taken away to be raised by the merchant's more powerful first wife. An-Mei's mother carefully plans a suicide ensuring that the rich man, afraid of her ghost, will take good care of An-Mei.

Lindo Jong explains her childhood in "The Red Candle," recounting her escape from an unfortunate marriage. Promised in marriage at two and delivered at twelve, Lindo Jong finds herself living with in-laws, whose only interest is grand-

The daughters in *The Joy Luck Club* (seen here in the film version) struggle to find a balance between the Chinese traditions embraced by their mothers and modern American ways. Pictured, from left to right: Rosaline Chao (Rose), Lauren Tom (Lena), Ming-Na Wen (June), and Tamlyn Tomita (Waverly).

children and an immature husband who doesn't love or desire her. Preying on the family's superstitions, Lindo invents a dream vision that foretells the destruction of the family if they do not release her from the marriage and supply her with enough money to emigrate to the United States. Once in America, she marries Tin Jong and has three children, one of whom is Waverly.

In "The Moon Lady," we meet Ying-Ying St. Clair. Her reminiscence is about a Moon Festival celebration at which she fell into Tai Lake. She is four and luckily rescued by strangers who leave her on the bank of the lake. Wandering the celebration grounds, she happens upon a play that tells the sad story of the wish-granting Moon Lady. At the end of the play, the Moon Lady agrees to grant a secret wish to everyone present. Ying-Ying approaches the actor to reveal her wish, only to discover that the lady is a man. She says that for a long time she forgot the details of that day, what she was going to ask and how her family found her. But as time has passed, she has recalled everything that happened that day "because it has happened many times in my life. The same innocence, trust, and restlessness, the wonder, fear and loneliness. How I lost myself [and how] I wished to be found."[10]

Twenty-Six Malignant Gates

The second part of the novel focuses on the American-born daughters of each club member. As a device for the reader to get to know them, each tells a significant story from her childhood. Waverly Jong recalls her time as a chess prodigy, how she learned to play the game by reading up on opening moves, the middle game, and the end game. She perfects these skills to become a national champion at age nine. This is also when she begins to tire of her mother's bragging and wants to break free of her mother's constant prodding. But she also worries about winning her mother's approval, a worry that carries on into adulthood even though she is the picture of success.

Lena St. Clair remembers a childhood filled with her mother's superstitions. When her mother becomes pregnant and loses the child, she has a nervous breakdown and retreats from family life. At the same time, Lena hears the Italian neighbors—mother and daughter—fighting. Initially, she is convinced that the girl has an unhappy life, but she comes to realize that the fighting is this family's way of expressing affection. In her home, however, her mother doesn't seem to see her at all, and Lena feels the burden of trying to make her mother come back to life.

Rose Hsu Jordan recollects the day her four-year-old brother drowned and her mother, once a religious person, lost her faith in God. Now, Rose is about to divorce her American husband, and her mother, despite losing faith, encourages Rose to try and save the marriage. "This is not hope. Not reason," An-Mei tells her. "This is your life, what you must do."[11] But she also says, "You must think for yourself, what you must do. If someone tells you, then you are not trying."

June's story is about her mother's pushing her to be a prodigy. As a child, June tries mightily to please her mother, culminating in a piano recital at which she fails miserably. June reflects that "unlike my [m]other, I did not believe I could be anything I wanted to be. I could only be me."[12] June has always lived in someone else's shadow. Suyuan always compared June to Waverly Jong, and June felt she simply couldn't live up to her mother's expectations: she was never a straight-A student, never excelled at anything. And her mother's foreignness always embarrassed her. Now that Suyuan is gone, however, June understands that her mother's wishes for her were really about giving her the confidence to be anything she wanted. Taking her mother's place at the mah-jongg table, June now realizes that the club is about preserving a way of life.

American Translation

In this third part of the novel, we learn about the conflicts the American-born Chinese women face as adults. We see the interplay of the Chinese values they were brought up with and the American ones they have inculcated—the "American circumstances and Chinese character" Lindo Jong refers to in speaking about her daughter.[13] Sometimes these work together and sometimes they do not.

Lena St. Clair describes her marital problems; she is married to her boss, who makes much more than she does, and yet he makes her pay half of all the household expenses. Waverly Jong worries about her mother's reaction to her Caucasian fiancé, only to realize that her mother has known all along and has accepted Waverly's choice. Rose comes to understand that she must fight for what she wants out of her divorce settlement and ultimately refuses to sign divorce papers, with conditions she does not accept. June recalls how, at the previous year's New Year's celebration, she fought with Waverly and how her mother, sensing her daughter's humiliation, gave her her own necklace with a special jade pendant. Suyuan tells June, "For a long time, I wanted to give you this necklace. See, I wore this on my skin, so when you put it on your skin, then you know my meaning. This is your life's importance."[14] She goes on to say that the jade is "young," but if worn every day the light green will turn darker. It's as if she is telling June that time and the shifting of one's viewpoint is not nearly as important as the mother-daughter bond, which is constant; that it is "life's importance."

Ying-Ying reflects on her younger self (portrayed here by Faye Yu) and resolves to stop her daughter from making the same mistakes that she herself has made.

Queen Mother of the Western Skies

We return to the club mothers, reflecting on their Chinese past and their American present. An-Mei Hsu begins by expressing her thoughts on her daughter's failing marriage, noting that by crying "No choice!" her daughter is in fact making a choice. She talks about the Chinese way of rearing girls, "to desire nothing, to swallow other people's misery, to eat [one's] own bitterness," is inextricably caught up with being born to this particular family of women: "All of us like stairs, one step after another, going up and down but all going the same way."[15] She remembers what it was like to move with her mother to the house of the rich merchant Wu Tsing. As one of his concubines, her mother has no power, and An-Mei is there to witness her mother's humiliation. Determined to end her suffering and to better her child's life, An-Mei's mother takes her own, two days before the lunar new year. An-Mei knows this is because she was planning her death "so carefully that it became a weapon."[16] "We both knew this: that on the third day after someone dies, the soul comes back to settle scores. In my mother's case, this would be the first day of the lunar new year. And because it is the new year, all debts must be paid, or disaster and misfortune will follow."[17] Thus, Wu Ting, fearful of vengeance, promises An-Mei's mother's ghost he will take care of An-Mei. Though her mother can do nothing in life, she ensures that her death will protect her daughter.

Ying-Ying St. Clair relives the abandonment of her first husband, whom she loved but who was a womanizer. For years after he leaves her, Ying-Ying floats "like a dead leaf on the water"[18] until she drifts out of her mother-in law's house and into a second cousin's home in the country outside Shanghai. She meets Clifford St. Clair while "working like a peasant"[19] in a clothing shop, and though she does not love him, she marries him when she learns that her first husband has died. She also notes that it was at this point she loses the fighting spirit she once had; she is "an unseen spirit." She has never told her daughter about her past and resolves to do so in order to save her daughter from repeating her mistakes.

Lindo Jong tells the next story. She starts by contrasting her daughter's growing up with her own Americanization. Of her daughter, she remarks, "She followed my Chinese ways only until she learned how to walk out the door by herself."[20] But she also sees their connection. As they peer at each other, faces together at the beauty salon, Lindo thinks, "These two faces, so much the same!"[21] She realizes that she too has been altered by her life in America. "Which one is better? If you show one, must you always sacrifice the other?"[22] She asks, "What did I lose? What did I get back in return?" And at long last, she decides to really talk to her daughter and ask what her daughter thinks.

The novel closes with a final story from June, who is traveling to China with her father to meet her half sisters. In a way, it is the culmination of all the Joy Luck Club members' experiences. After years of refusing her Chinese background, she now embraces it. For the first time, it seems, she asks her father about the meaning of her Chinese name, Jing-mei. He tells her "'Jing' like excellent *jing*. Not just good, it's something pure, essential, the best quality. *Jing* is good leftover stuff when you take impurities out of something like gold, or rice, or salt. So what is left—just pure essence. And 'Mei' this is common *mei*, as in *meimei*, 'younger sister.'"[23] She understands that her mother meant her to be the essence of her older half sisters. As individuals, June sees no common features but understands they are connected: "I also see what part of me is Chinese.

It is so obvious. It is my family. It is in our blood. After all these years, it can finally be let go." And finally, June understand that "[t]ogether we look like our mother. Her same eyes, her same mouth, open in surprise to see, at last, her long-cherished wish."[24]

Structure

The novel is composed of sixteen stories in four sections. Many reviewers have found significance in this number. For example, critic Mary Ellen Snodgrass calls the book's structure a "mathematically precise plot revealed in sixteen chapters."[25] The talk-story style of each chapter is interesting because Tan and her agent originally envisioned the book as a collection of short stories. According to Tan, the structure of the novel has more to do with the publisher and her agent's decisions than with any hidden meanings. "Originally there were going to be five sections of the book, three stories for each of the five elements found in harmonious nature: earth, fire, wood, water and metal. But my agent, Sandy Dijkstra, thought that my five-part structure was too contrived and I realized that five families made for a more difficult balancing act."[26] Nonetheless, Tan's remark indicates that she does think about symbolism, to some extent, in the five elements she originally conceived.

Themes

Tan does not like reviewers and educators to assume that her personal stories represent all Asian Americans. While it would be untrue to say that Tan's only focus is about the collision of two cultures, it definitely has informed her life and her writing. Often, though writers may not set out to use specific metaphors or symbols, readers find them; one of the joys of reading is that readers bring their own life experiences to a written work. Though Amy Tan writes about universal concerns like family relationships and self-identity, she also writes about "members of an ethnic minority that has over a century or more developed, a distinctive *diaspora* [scattering or movement of people from their homeland]. Culture that exists within the larger framework of cultures that is known as the United States."[27]

Identity

As noted, a prominent theme of *The Joy Luck Club* is the idea of personal identity and what it means to live between two cultures; to be American and foreign at the same time. Auntie Lindo says in her story, "Double Face," that "It's my fault Waverly is this way. I wanted my children to have the best combination: American circumstances and Chinese character. How could I know these things do not mix?"[28]

Each Chinese mother has high hopes for her daughter; they should be "American strong" while at the same time, obedient. Each daughter has to find her own identity, but also has to find a way to compromise with her mother's ideal.

Tan makes use of Chinese superstitions, often filtered through an American's eye. According to one critic, "Tan's ties to China have so much to do with her mother. When Tan's brother and father became terminally ill with brain tumors, her mother called on as many of the Chinese religious traditions that she could. Tan describes her mother as "haunted"

metaphor

A word or phrase used to compare one thing to another in order to show a similarity.

symbol

Something that stands for or represents another thing.

by these spirits that she so strongly believed in."[29] Tan says she prefers to write in images rather than symbols, and that if she does use symbols in her work, they are "carefully nudged out of their hiding places by others. I don't consciously place symbols in such a clever fashion as some students have given me credit for."[30] In other words, she does not consciously use superstitions as a device for her characters to get in touch with themselves.

Choice and Fate

All their lives, the Joy Luck Club mothers have struggled with cultural expectations of obedience and conformity while wanting to make their own decisions and establish their own identities. Suyuan Woo takes charge of her own destiny when she forms the Joy Luck Club in Kweilin during the Japanese invasion. Others around her and her friends criticize the club members for being indulgent: "People thought we were wrong to serve banquets every week while many people in the city were starving, eating rats and, later the garbage that the poorest rats used to feed on. Others thought we were possessed by demons—to celebrate when even within our own families we had lost generations, had lost homes and fortunes, and were separated husband from wife, brother from sister, daughter from mother. How could we laugh, people asked." It was not that they didn't have misery or fear, recalled Suyuan, rather she felt it was worse to "sit and wait for our own deaths with proper somber faces."[31] The Joy Luck Club was Suyuan's way of pretending "each week had become the new year," a way of dealing with the chaos around them by providing a place for the members to talk and forget themselves and their problems. "Their hope for luck was their joy."[32]

By continuing the club in the United States, its members find a way to settle themselves in a new culture. The mothers want their daughters to be active participants in their own fate, but they find it hard to be open enough about their own pasts to give any meaningful advice. Perhaps Ying-Ying St. Clair is the exception. As she sees her daughter's unhappy marriage, she confronts her own troubling past and resolves to help her. "I will use sharp pain," she tells us "to penetrate my daughter's tough skin and cut her tiger spirit lose. She will fight me, because this is the nature of two tigers. But I will win and give her my spirit, because this is the way a mother loves her daughter."[33]

Clashing Cultures

In *The Joy Luck Club*, there exists a clash between cultures and generations. "As important as the Joy Luck Club is to the immigrant mothers, their daughters find its existence perplexing and embarrassing."[34] They will eat Chinese food or celebrate the Chinese New Year, but they want to leave these traditions in their childhood homes. When in public, they may look Chinese but they make American choices. They do not understand how important the club is; in fact, June recalls thinking that "Joy Luck was a shameful Chinese custom, like the secret gathering of the Ku Klux Klan or the tom-tom dances of TV Indians."[35] For the mothers, Joy Luck is about preserving a cultural heritage for themselves and for their daughters. As Huntley explains, "Only through the intervention of the Joy Luck Club aunties are the daughters, represented by Jing-Mei, able to finally hear their mothers' stories, to reconcile the two disparate worlds of their heritage and to receive symbolically the gift of the swan feather."[36]

The film version of *The Joy Luck Club* was generally well-received by audiences, and Tan declared herself satisfied with the project.

Joy Luck at the Movies

Amy Tan did not originally want to make *The Joy Luck Club* into a movie. "I had numerous people interested in optioning the book, but I had heard horror stories. I was nervous about the possibility of someone making something really horrible. That the old myth of selling my soul to the devil would come true. And I'd be ashamed of it. And I'd have to kill myself publicly to make amends."[37] But director Wayne Wang was inducted into the project and it was a perfect match: he was born in Hong Kong, based in San Francisco, and understood not only film-making but the immigrant experience as well.

Screenwriter Ron Bass joined the team, and they worked together in a way almost unprecedented in Hollywood where "[i]t's common practice in Hollywood for screenwriters to savage each other's work and plot to get the lion's share of the screen credits. But Tan and Bass insist theirs was a true collaboration. They critiqued and revised each other's scripts, then locked themselves into a hotel room and wrote dialogue together."[38] Once the script was completed, they went to find a studio with the condition that they would all be coproducers. After shopping around, they found Walt Disney Studios, who agreed to make the movie.

The Joy Luck Club opened in theaters on September 8, 1993, and met with mixed reviews. Tan makes a brief cameo appearance in the film, along with a family photo of her deceased father and brother.

Adolescent girls in the United States may clash violently with their mothers on any number of issues. But in this case, that developmental stage is compounded by the Chinese mothers' fear that their daughters will not have Chinese "character." Despite these worries, the daughters become adults, and their mothers' dreams come true to some extent. Through June, the Joy Luck Club survives, and "joy luck" (namely, the hope for happiness despite misfortune) prevails.[39]

Food

Food is a recurring theme in this and in other works of Amy Tan. According to critic Huntley, food imagery crops up in each narrative and links the past, present, and future. Food also becomes a vehicle for the mothers to share experiences with their daughters.

As the novel opens, June remembers that her mother was supposed to be hosting this club meeting and that Lindo had served red bean soup at the last one. June knows that her mother was going to prepare black sesame soup, because in addition to being a mah-jongg gathering, the Joy Luck Club is also a bit of a culinary battleground. At the end of the novel, when June and her father visit China, their first meal with relatives is room service: hamburgers, French fries, and apple pie with ice cream; standard fare in the United States. Thus, food is a way to connect generations and families.

imagery

The use of language to create an image, or a picture in the reader's mind, about how something looks, sounds or feels.

By describing food, the mothers can also reveal some of their history. When Lindo Jong narrates the story of her first marriage, she recalls seeing her first husband-to-be at the red-egg ceremonies where baby boys are named. When she is sent to live with her in-laws, her first job is to chop vegetables. Her first husband uses the soup to express his displeasure. Lindo cooks her husband's breakfast every morning and attends to her mother-in-law's evening meal. In the same way, Ying-Ying St. Clair remembers the Moon Festival. She remembers the day's provisions in detail, a hamper full of apples, pomegranates, pears, preserved meats and vegetables, and mooncakes and more.[40] For An-Mei, food evokes more painful memories; for example, when a steaming pot of soup falls from the table and scalds her or when her mother returns to nurse her dying grandmother and cooks a soup into which she adds her own flesh.

Food is also a way to show cultural incompatibility. When Waverly brings her Caucasian fiancé, Rich, to her parents' for dinner, he blunders miserably. He drinks too much, helps himself to too much food before anyone else, and fails to sample every dish with requisite politeness. Furthermore, he dumps soy sauce over Lindo's prized steamed pork and preserved vegetable dish, which horrifies Lindo. Rich has no idea what he has done, and Waverly cannot begin to explain it to him.

4 The Kitchen God's Wife

Two years after the wild success of her first novel, Tan published *The Kitchen God's Wife*. It was not so much a second novel as one of many attempts after her first book to write another novel. In total, Amy Tan "started and abandoned—seven potential novels" before completing the eighth manuscript that become her second book.[1]

As in *The Joy Luck Club*, Tan writes of women and daughters and their relationships, as well as clashes between cultures. But here, the focus is more on the mother's story. In fact, according to the biography Huntley wrote, "Amy Tan has said on a number of occasions that *The Kitchen God's Wife* is her mother's story."[2]

Plot

The novel has two plot lines: one set in present-day United States involving Pearl Louie Brandt and her mother, Winnie (Jiang Weili), the other in preCommunist China. In that story line, we are taken back in time as Winnie endures a horrible marriage, loses three children to illness, lives through World War II, and then finally reaches America to create a successful life.

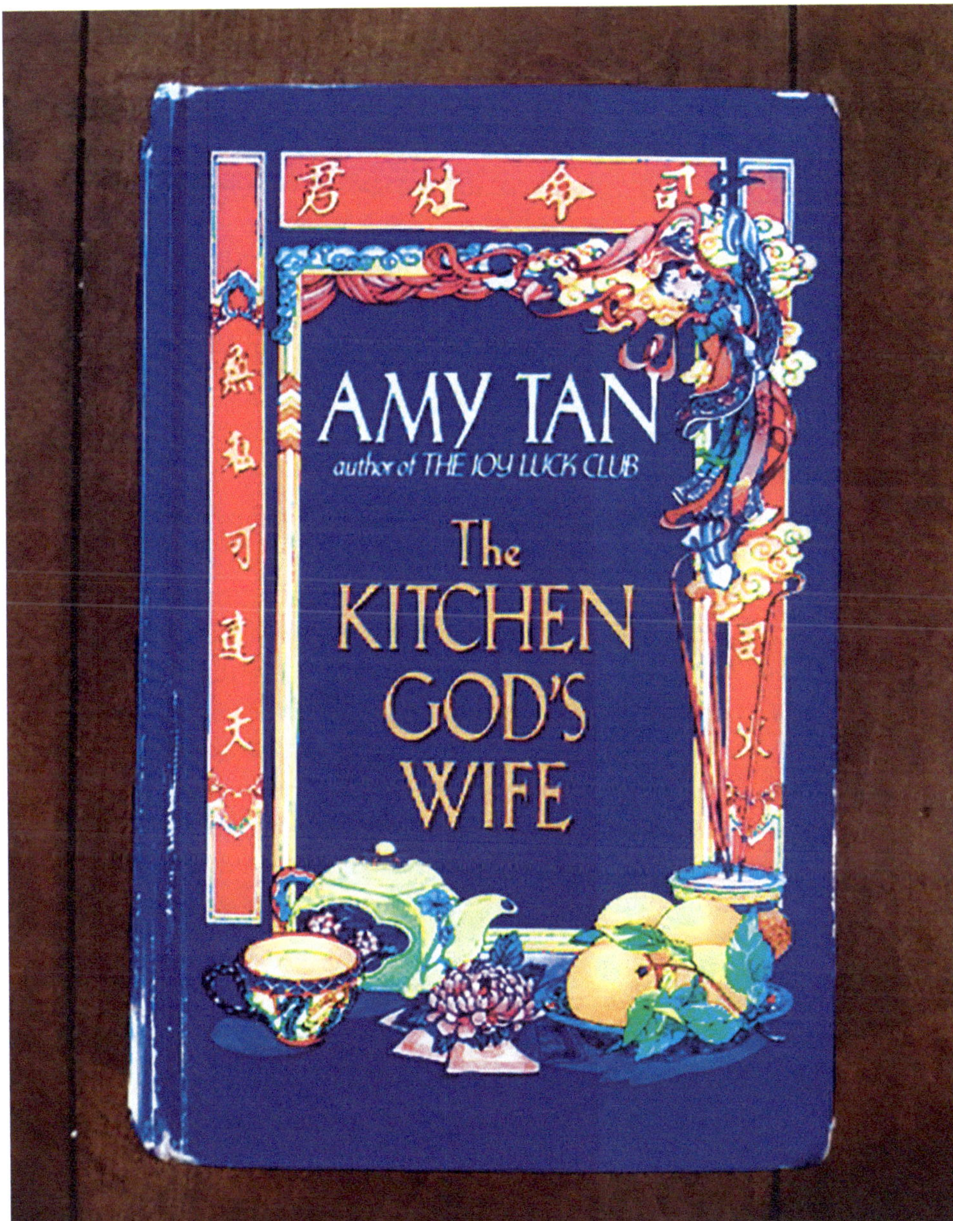

The Kitchen God's Wife was published in 1991 and, like *The Joy Luck Club*, it contained some autobiographical elements.

SINO-JAPANESE CONFLICT (1894–1895)

Relations between China and Japan have never been easy. In 1894, Japan wanted to dominate Korea, a country that had been allied with China. Because of its location and its resources of coal and iron, Japan was able to force Korea into trade agreements and declare itself independent from China. Japan had been modernizing since the mid-1800s; Korea identified with forward-thinking ideas, while China backed the more conservative royal government.

In 1894, pro-Japanese Korean leader Kim Ok-kyun was called to Shanghai and assassinated. His corpse was shipped back to Korea and publicly dismembered as a warning to any other rebels. The Japanese were outraged, and later in the year, full rebellion broke out in Korea. At the request of the Korean king, China sent troops, which the Japanese considered a violation of a previous agreement by the two nations to keep their troops out of Korea (Li-Ito Convention). When war between China and Japan was declared on August 1, 1894, it was assumed that China would easily win because of the size of its army. However, Japan had a much more modern military and was better equipped and prepared. By March 1895, the Japanese had conquered Shandong province, and Manchuria and ruled the sea approaches to Beijing. The Chinese were ready to make peace.

To end the war, China had to agree to recognize Korea as an independent country. It also had to give up Taiwan and part of Manchuria. But China's defeat had even deeper consequences. Western powers were encouraged to make further demands from the Chinese government, such as opening up trade in China. Within China itself, the growing discontent with the government that had gotten the country into war marked the beginnings of a revolution that would topple the existing dynasty and change China forever.[3]

An illustration depicts the 1894 Battle of Ping-Yang during the Sino-Japanese conflict.

As the novel begins, we meet Pearl Louie Brandt, an American-born Chinese woman who seems to have nothing to do with her Chinese culture and is always at odds with her mother. "Whenever my mother talks to me, she begins the conversation as if we were already in the middle of an argument,"[4] says Pearl from the very beginning. But theirs is no ordinary argument. As Pearl narrates the first two chapters we learn that she is married and has two children of her own, yet her mother still has a profound effect on her. Winnie's bossiness and belief in superstitions have created a distance between the two women to the point where Pearl's husband, Phil, believes Pearl is "driven by blind devotion to fear and guilt."[5] From Winnie's point of view they are "always careful to be polite, always trying not to bump into each other, just like strangers."[6]

We also learn that Pearl has multiple sclerosis and that every time she has attempted to tell Winnie, her mother interrupts with some other concern. It's as if Winnie is afraid to hear what Pearl has to say, and Pearl is afraid to include her mother in her adult life. However, a cousin's engagement and an elderly aunt's funeral require Pearl to come home, and it's then that Pearl hears her mother's story and begins to understand the root of their uneasy relationship.

In chapter two, Winnie tells Pearl's daughters about the Kitchen God: "In China a long time ago, there was a rich farmer named Zhang, such a lucky man. Fish jumped in his river, pigs grazed his land, ducks flew around his yard as thick as clouds. And that was because he was blessed with a hardworking wife named Guo."[7] Zhang takes up with another woman, who chases Guo away, and then squanders all of Zhang's riches until he is left with nothing. Zhang becomes so poor, he crawls "from the grate of one household to another crying, 'Give me your moldy grain.'"[8] He is taken in by a kind woman, but then he finds out that this woman is Guo. So he jumps into the kitchen fireplace to hide his shame and though Guo tries to put out the flames, his ashes "fly up to heave in three puffs of smoke."

Once in heaven, Zhang meets the Jade Emperor, who declares that for having the courage to admit he was wrong, Zhang is now Kitchen God, watching over everyone's behavior. Each year it is his duty to let the Jade Emperor know who deserves good luck and who deserves bad. When Pearl suggests that putting one's faith in the Kitchen God is an easy way to get luck, Winnie remarks, "Why should I want that kind of person to judge me, a man who cheated his wife? His wife was the good one, not him."[9]

Some critics have suggested that by introducing the Kitchen God here, Tan sets up a parallel between the god and Winnie's first husband, Wen Fu, who we learn in subsequent chapters is a cruel man and, like Zhang, takes up with other women. Critics also suggest that by presenting the story this way, Tan creates a relationship between personal and historical; the way Winnie's domineering first husband treats her and his family is like Japan's treatment of Chinese during the Sino-Japanese War (1937–1945).[10]

Beginning with chapter three, Winnie takes over the narrative. She begins by describing Helen (Hulan), a woman who for years Winnie has called her sister-in-law. Helen is foolish, Winnie says, but she is also lucky. As an example, she recounts how Helen bought a three-day-old fish on sale that she thought was bad but that turned out to be quite tasty. Winnie, on the other hand, buys a very expensive special fish that makes her husband sick enough to go to the hospital and saddles them with huge bills. By recounting this anecdote,

Tan makes Winnie (and the reader) consider the interplay of luck, fate, and choice. Winnie herself isn't sure how these forces play out in her life. She says, "If my life had been that way, one thing leading to another, then I could look back and I would know the lessons of my life; the fate that was given me, the choices I took, the mistakes that are mine. And perhaps I would still have time to change my luck."[11]

We learn that Winnie could have married a man called Lin, but he was persuaded by an aunt not to because the family was not very rich. Years later, she meets this man and his wife in her husband's church in Fresno, California, and realizes that she can view her life as "the way it happened" and "the way it did not."[12] In other words, she understands that there are always choices in life, even if it does not seem like it. Added to choice are the complications of fate and luck. Winnie asks, "Was it fate . . . or was it because I didn't know I had a choice?" A simple "yes" or "no" can determine a whole lifetime, and yet as Winnie notices, "How can you know [what choice] is good and what is bad until you have tasted it?"[13]

Winnie explains that for forty years, she has introduced Helen as her sister-in-law, but that this has been a lie. In fact, her brother was only a half brother and died before World War II. Winnie describes how other family members altered this brother's fate to suit their needs. "[M]y half brother went on to have many other lives. When the Japanese took over Shanghai in 1937, my uncle pretended to welcome them to his textile shop. My own nephew was educated in Japan, and now lives in Changsha, married to a Japanese girl. And then my half brother took on another life. When the Japanese lost in 1945 and the Kuomintang came back, my uncle said, 'My poor nephew, Kun, he was a Kuomintang hero. Died in

Changsha.'"[14] It is as though Tan is demonstrating how the past can be changed.

In telling her story, Winnie recalls the prewar Shanghai of her youth with its roots in feudal China and its ties to European culture, a place caught between the old and the new.[15] We learn that she lost her mother early (as actually happened to Daisy Tan), and that her first marriage ended disastrously. At eighteen, Winnie married Wen Fen, a handsome man whose family were merchants. Initially, Wen Fen was interested in Winnie's cousin Peanut, but after discovering Winnie's family was wealthier, he convinces his family to hire a marriage broker and set up the marriage between him and Winnie. Completely unaware of the reason for his change of heart, Winnie accepts the proposal.

anecdote

A brief story about something that happens to a person.

Like any new bride, she is nervous and unsure. Just before the wedding, Winnie's cousin tells her that the Wen family have made their money selling the paintings and sacred family objects of country families who are in dire circumstances and must part with their things just to stay alive. "True they make a lot money. Foreigners love those paintings. But it is riches made from someone else's tragedy. The reason why they had to sell, that's one kind of tragedy. But the worst tragedy is still to come . . . when the Wens die and try to go to the next world, you can be sure all those people's ancestors will be standing at the front gate, ready to kick them out."[16] Winnie does not want to believe this and makes a point of how innocent she was, not always a negative person. "When I was young, I wanted to believe in something good. And when that good started to go away I still wanted to grab it, make it stay."[17] But as events

Winnie's story takes the reader back to Shanghai, China, before World War II. This photograph was taken around 1930.

unfold, she finds out her husband has lied and assumed his dead brother's identity to pose as an army pilot. On top of being dishonest, he is cruel, even sadistic with Winnie. "I now felt as if my husband were two people. One dead, one alive. One true, one false [. . .]I tried to be a proper wife. I tried to love the half of him that was not so bad."[18]

Winnie first meets Helen when, as the wives of pilots, they are stationed in Hangchow. Even though the women are opposites—Helen is loud, brash, and poor, while Winnie is well-bred and submissive—they are brought together by circumstances. They experience the hardships of the war together and eventually move to California and start their new lives together.

As in *The Joy Luck Club*, women are friends and foes at the same time. Winnie observes that her and Helen's friendship has always had "four splits and five cracks,"[19] that is, there is always some tension between them. Nevertheless, they have a history surviving the war and their circumstances; they depend on one another. Confiding their deepest secrets: that Helen's first husband had actually been involved with her sister (who died while trying to deliver an illegitimate child), and that Winnie's daughter Pearl is actually the result of her first husband's rape; fate has fused the two together.

Structure

In this novel, Tan lets the main characters speak for themselves, retelling the important events in their lives as they remember them. Winnie narrates most of the novel as she reveals to her daughter how she transformed from Jiang Winnie to Winnie. In the first two chapters, Tan lets Pearl lay the groundwork by describing the uneasy relationship between her and her mother. She also introduces Helen (Hulan) Kwong, her

The History Behind Winnie and Suyuan's Stories

Conflicts between China and Japan continued into the twentieth century as the Japanese continued to covet Chinese land. Because there was turmoil inside China between the Communists and the Nationalists (Kuomintang), Japan caught the country off guard. On the night of July 7, 1937, Japanese and Chinese troops clashed ten miles west of Beijing. Using the conflict as an excuse, the Japanese launched a full-scale invasion, quickly catching strategic cities in Northern China. Advancing west and south, the Japanese won Jinan (the capital of Shandong) and then Nanjing (where Winnie and Suyuan are). Within a year, Japan held all of China's major industrial cities and much of its best farmland. In June 1938, the Japanese tried to seize a railroad junction near the Yellow River. Nationalist Chinese leader Chiang Kai Shek made the decision to blow up the river's dikes, causing a massive flood that set back the Japanese as it killed many of their soldiers and destroyed supplies and armory. It also destroyed four thousand Chinese villages and thousands of Chinese peasants.[20]

mother's oldest friend, "whose own story intersects with Winnie's story and whose decision to reveal long-hidden truths precipitates both Winnie's epic confession and Pearl's revelations."[21]

As Winnie's story unfolds, we are reminded that it is a story being told out loud in the present when Winnie asks Pearl a question or makes a comment about something current. "Critics commend Tan's ability to create unique voices for Pearl and Winnie."[22] When Winnie speaks, her words and syntax sound and read just as one would expect from a person whose first language is not English. By contrast, Pearl sounds "American."

Themes

Silence

As a woman raised in male-dominated, prerevolutionary China, Winnie has learned to be quiet, to silently accept suffering. As E. D. Huntley notes, the effects of silence can be "misunderstanding, loneliness and isolation, erasure and invisibility, depression, madness, even death."[23] Even though she has moved to the United States, Winnie is still prey to oppression. Her habit of silence has affected her relationship with her daughter, with the result that both of them lose "a shared history and a common emotional language"; they are strangers to one another.[24] When someone does not share his or her story, they allow others to construct it for them, giving others power over them.

For almost forty years, Winnie has kept her story from Pearl and used Helen to help her hide her history. But when Helen threatens to tell Pearl herself, it forces Winnie and Pearl to use their own voices to connect with one another. Until Winnie can tell Pearl her story, Pearl does not know her, assuming only that she is strange and superstitious. Being brought up in the United States, Pearl does not have the same connection to China and is frustrated by her mother's "various hypotheses, the way religion, medicine and superstition, all merge with her own beliefs. Pearl adds, "According to my mother, *nothing* is an accident. She's like a Chinese version of Freud, or worse."[25] Winnie can't understand her daughter either. While straightening Pearl's childhood room, she recalls that she and her daughter have always tried to sidestep difficult conversations: "That is how she is. That is how I am. Always careful to be polite, always trying not to bump into each other, just like strangers."[26]

Food

As in *The Joy Luck Club*, food transports the reader to the China of the 1920s and 1930s in which the characters once lived. Winnie's mother wears Western dresses and Chinese robes, and likes English biscuits,[27] as well as a special small fish called *wah-wah-yu*. Knowing Winnie's mother's taste in food gives us extra insight, and we can see how she represents tradition and innovation.

When we read about the engagement party and wedding of Helen's son, the meals described are notably elaborate meals. Also, the way Helen and Winnie argue about the food is really a way of doing what they always do—making a connection. Food highlights the difference between the first generation and their American-born children. For example, Helen and Winnie's daughters don't cook Chinese food. And Pearl's children aren't even familiar with much of it.

Food also serves as a link between past and present. Recalling the day her mother left, Winnie tells Pearl about the bowl of *syen do jang* (salty soy-milk soup) the servant brought

A Chinese-American family enjoys a traditional Chinese meal at a San Francisco restaurant. Food plays an important role in Tan's work, representing tradition and family.

Food in China

Cuisine of varied geography. According to author Charles Benn, "It is probably fair to say that the Chinese have been the most omnivorous people in the history of the world."[28] There are many reasons for this. First, China covers a large and geographically diverse area: Inner Mongolia is grassland, while the part of China closest to Vietnam is humid and tropical. There are the fish-rich seacoasts of the Pacific and fertile plains on the border with Tibet. Another reason is the Chinese tradition of searching for "substances that could cure illness, prolong life and confer immortality."[29] Still another reason may be an early passion for something exotic. Some foods, such as bear's paw, "reached the table because they were hard to obtain," were imported, or were difficult to acquire.[30]

Cuisine of history. In China, food has significance beyond sustenance. The Chinese philosopher Confucius believed that enjoying food was an ingredient for peace and harmony. He established "culinary standards and proper table etiquette"[31] still followed today. For example, meals must be balanced (fan/t'sai). Fan (starches and grains) should be equalin proportion to meat and vegetables (t'sai). Hot and cold foods should be balanced and there should be harmony between "the five flavors" —bitter, hot, sour, salty and sweet. Dim sum is an excellent illustration. Dating back to the Sung

Dynasty (960–1279), the phrase means "touch the heart," and refers to the way in which royal chefs would try to invent dishes that appealed to royal palates, as well as to touch their hearts. Dim sum includes a variety of items, both sweet and savory. Each dish reflects "the artistry of the chef and may include steamed shrimp dumplings (har gao), steamed pork and shrimp dumplings (siu mai), spring rolls (cheun gyun), steamed barbecued pork buns (cha siu bau), rice noodle rolls (cheong fun), green pepper stuffed with shrimp (yern chang chew), and congee (jook). More exotic dishes include chicken feet (fung jow and curried squid (ca lay yao yue). Desserts range from sesame seed balls (gee ma gyun) to egg custard tart (dan tat). Potstickers (guo tie), which are often served, are northern Chinese in origin, and not considered traditional."[32]

Cuisine of practicality. Until recently, food, the fuel for cooking it, and water were not plentiful in China. Much of Chinese cuisine has evolved around this fact; anything that took a long time or a lot of fuel was not practical. To wit, one of the most distinctive ways of cooking is stir-frying (chao). This involves cutting everything into small pieces and briefly stirring them at high heat so that cooking is quick. Steaming is another common technique in Chinese cooking. This is economical because small plates of food can be steamed on top of boiling rice and stacked on top of each other.

her that morning (noteworthy that it's the same concoction that Pearl's daughter Cleo loves).[33] When Helen suggests a new Chinese restaurant that serves fried eel and chives, Winnie says no. Eels remind her of her past and of the atrocities of the war between China and Japan. In recounting her distaste she asks, "Why do some memories live only on your tongue or in your nose? Why do others always stay in your heart?"[34]

Memory and Truth

By telling stories, Winnie and Pearl share their secrets and, as Huntley notes, keep the past alive while at the same time, changing their relationship to it. "Can you imagine how innocent I was," Winnie asks Pearl when retelling the story of her wedding day.

Tan also explores the nature of memory. While telling Pearl her story, Winnie often mentions that Helen is incorrect in her perceptions: "Helen always tells me, 'Why do you think about those old things? Useless to regret. You cannot change the past.' She doesn't remember. She and I have changed the past many times, for many reasons."[35] Winnie herself admits that memories can change. Describing the few memories she has of her mother, Winnie says, "I remember her ten thousand different ways [. . .] I have been thinking about my mother for almost seventy years, so it must be ten thousand different times. And it must be that she has changed ten thousand different ways, each time I recalled her. So maybe my memory of her is not right anymore."[36]

In this novel, we get the perspective of Winnie, Helen, and Pearl but which is true? By using the talk-story as a vehicle, Tan is able to represent multiple points of view, thus illustrating how there is no such thing as an "objective" truth: Says Winnie, "ten thousand different things that come from your memory or imagination—and you do not know which is which, which was true, which is false."[37]

Choice, Fate, and Luck

Throughout the novel, Tan examines the role of luck and fate and choice: "What in our lives is fate, the circumstances we're born into, and what are the things that we have really chosen at those important turns in our lives?"[38] As a writer, Tan says she takes all these disparate events and connects them. "I have to make them seem inevitable and yet surprising and plausible [. . .] I have the luxury to do exactly what it is we all need time to do, and that is just think about the mystery of life."[39]

As a woman growing up in prerevolutionary China, Winnie does not have many choices. But she realizes what taking a chance could mean: "Chance is the first step you take, luck is what comes afterward [. . .] if you get bad luck, then you need to take another chance to turn things from bad to good."[40] She embraces superstitions; for example, when she, Helen, and their husbands arrive in Kunming, Winnies says, "Wen Fu and I received the worst rooms, both of them facing a bad-luck direction."[41] Winnie believes that her first child was stillborn because she dropped scissors on the floor and remembered a relative telling her about the bad luck of dropping scissors.[42] At the same time, Winnie is constantly questioning superstitions and the notion of fate and truth, as when she disdains the idea that a character like the Kitchen God should judge her, or when she remarks that Helen twists everything around so she has to "argue with myself to what is really true."[43] Perhaps because she thinks Pearl might find fault with her, Winnie blames her bad luck: "I will tell you when all my luck changed, from bad to worse. You tell me if this was my fault"[44] and points out that because her own mother died long ago, there was no one to guide her, particularly in choosing a husband.

By telling her story, Winnie is reliving her youth with an eye toward determining how luck, fate, and choice become intertwined. She realizes there is no easy answer: "If I try to say what happened my story would not flow forward like a river from the beginning to the end, everything connected, the lake to the sea. If my life had been that way, one thing leading to another, then I could look back and I would know the lessons of my life; the fate that was given me, the choices I took, the mistakes that are mine. And perhaps I would still have time to change my luck."[45] Later, she asks "Was it fate . . . or was it because I didn't know I had a choice?"[46]

The Bonesetter's Daughter

In 2001, Amy Tan's fourth novel was published. Like her other novels, *The Bonesetter's Daughter* examines the relationship between mothers and daughters, as well as cross-cultural identity. "It tells the tale of three generations of women: how they loved, how they suffered, and how they survived."[1]

Though not as well-known as *The Joy Luck Club* or *The Kitchen God's Wife*, *The Bonesetter's Daughter* received its share of praise. It was named a Notable Book by the *New York Times* and nominated for the Baileys Women's Prize for Fiction (until 2013 known as the Orange Prize). The Baileys Women's Prize is awarded to the woman who, in the opinion of the judges, has written the best full-length novel in English; it is one of the most prestigious prizes for literature in the United Kingdom. It was also made into an opera that debuted in San Francisco in the fall of 2008. It featured a "Western-Chinese fusion score" by Stewart Wallace, a composer friend of Tan's, and a libretto [words set to a score] by Tan.

Plot

Covering two continents and one hundred years of history, The *Bonesetter's Daughter* begins with a prologue entitled "Truth." In it, the central character, LuLing Young, recounts her early life in a village just outside Peking (Beijing) called Immortal Heart. When she was six, she recalls, her nurse, Precious Auntie, would help her bathe every morning before

Tan poses in her New York City apartment in 2001, around the time that *The Bonesetter's Daughter* was released.

proceeding to the ancestral hall to pray. Because she is mute, Precious Auntie uses her hands to speak with LuLing. Precious Auntie explains her family's name, "the name of all the bonesetters,"[2] and admonishes LuLing to never forget it. At the time, LuLing does not realize it but it is her name, too.

Fast-forward to present-day San Francisco, where LuLing and her adult daughter, Ruth, try to understand and reconcile their differences. When the novel opens, Ruth is coping with having lost her voice for a week. This same laryngitis has afflicted Ruth every year in August, and she wonders about its genesis. Could it be psychological, or as her superstitious Chinese mother believes, a sign of ghosts? It would certainly stand to reason if the malady were psychosomatic, meaning that it is caused by mental or emotional problems rather than by physical illness. Ruth and her boyfriend are not really getting along, and his two teenage daughters are rude and snappish to her. To top it off, her mother, with whom relations have always been touchy, is beginning to be forgetful and testy. Ruth accompanies her mother to a checkup where the doctor cannot say what ails LuLing—he suggests that it may be depression but that to be sure, he will run more tests.

flashback

A way of relating the present story to something that happened before the story takes place. Dreams and memories are a way of incorporating flashbacks into a story.

Meanwhile, Ruth takes care of things in her home as well as for her mother. Through a series of flashbacks, we learn more about the relationship between mother and daughter. "Being the only child of a widow, Ruth had always been forced to serve as LuLing's mouthpiece. By the time she was ten, Ruth was the English-speaking 'Mrs LuLing Young' on the telephone, the one who made appointments for the doctor, wrote letters to the bank."[3] This reliance on her daughter begins to extend to other things, like shopping and investment advice, and ultimately to believing that Ruth can communicate with the ghosts of the dead. One night, LuLing becomes convinced that Ruth is channeling the spirit of Precious Auntie, about whose death she has always felt guilty. Posing as Precious Auntie, Ruth reassures her mother that she is not cursed.

Ruth organizes the annual family get-together during the Full Moon Festival, an intimate gathering of close family and friends. However, Ruth's boyfriend, Art, insists that she invite his ex-wife and her new family. Ruth does so, even though she's angry about it, feeling that it is further evidence that her boyfriend does not value what is important to her. Toward the end of the meal, Ruth passes out presents. She gives both her mother and her Auntie GaoLing pictures of what she assumes are them as girls standing on either side of their mother. But LuLing insists that it is not her real mother, and that GaoLing is her sister-in law. Her real mother, she says, is Precious Auntie. This sends Ruth into a tailspin, convinced that her mother is really losing touch with reality.

After more testing and another visit to the doctor's office, Ruth's fears are confirmed: her mother has Alzheimer's disease, a degeneriative condition in which one's body can be healthy and strong but one's mind does not work properly, resulting in disorientation, mood swings, and personality changes. Ruth tries to explain this diagnosis to her mother, but LuLing insists her memory is fine. It becomes clear that LuLing can no longer perform daily household tasks, but when Ruth tries to hire in-home help, LuLing sends every aide away. Ruth realizes that LuLing cannot be left alone and so begins to stay with her in her apartment. This means that she must miss her vacation with Art, even as she feels a growing distance between

The Chinatown section of San Francisco serves as the setting for the first part of *The Bonesetter's Daughter*.

them. When LuLing wanders away from home at night, Ruth calls upon Auntie Gaoling and asks her to keep her mother for a week so she can clean her mother's apartment and see to finishing her own freelance writing contracts.

In the final chapter of the novel's first section, Ruth falls into a reverie about her childhood when she finds the diary she kept as a preteen. She recalls her misunderstanding about sex, the beginning of her friendship with Wendy, a woman with whom she is still close, and the time that her mother tried to commit suicide. Ruth recalls that as a teen, her mother snooped in her diary and, incensed, she writes in her diary so that her mother will see it: "I hate her!" and "You talk about killing yourself, so why don't you ever do it? I wish you would. Just do it, do it, do it!"[4] Instead of talking about this with her daughter, LuLing falls out a window and ends up in the hospital. Ruth knows it is the result of reading the words in her diary, but the two never discuss it.

On Ruth's sixteenth birthday, her mother presents her with "a black book and a tiny purse of red silk, fastened with a miniature frog clasp."[5] Inside that purse is a jade ring Ruth has always wanted. The book turns out to be a bible in Chinese but inside that bible is a black-and-white photo of a young Chinese woman who, LuLing informs Ruth, is her mother. Then LuLing takes back these gifts because "some things too good use right now. Save for later 'preciate more."[6] Of course, this makes Ruth mad, especially because she loved the jade ring.

Tan brings us back to the present, where Ruth continues to clean her mother's apartment. "A thought ran through her mind: The photo her mother kept in the Bible. She had also said that was her mother. Who was in that picture?"[7] Combing through her mother's old hiding places, Ruth finds the bible, and realizes it contains the same photo her mother showed at the family reunion, claiming that Precious Auntie was her mother. She also finds a second copy of her mother's memoir, but this one is different. The copy her mother gave her begins with, "These are the things I know are true." This copy begins "These are the things I should not forget." Ruth resolves to get a translator, compare the two versions, and above all, get her mother to talk about her life.

The second part of the novel is told from LuLing's perspective, the way she wrote it down in the memoir Ruth has found. We learn that LuLing's mother is Precious Auntie, the daughter of a famous bonesetter. Precious Auntie was to marry the youngest boy of the powerful Liu clan named Baby Uncle, but a rival suitor, Chang, kills Baby Uncle and Precious Auntie's father on their way to the wedding. Wild with grief, Precious Auntie swallows hot resin which disfigures her and renders her mute. She is pregnant by Baby Uncle and because she has no one else, Great-Granny Liu decides that Precious Auntie can stay with the Lius. However, the baby will be given to Mother, and Precious Auntie will be the baby's nurse. To anyone who asks, the family will say that Precious Auntie is a "distant relation from Peking, a cousin who lived in a nunnery until it burned down and took you with it."[8] We also learn that Mother's real child is GaoLing, whose birth date is falsified so that everyone can live without scandal.

In the following chapter, we discover that the village where LuLing has grown up is where archaeologists discover Peking Man. Hoping for more bones, the archaeologists are willing to pay to get them. Because her father was a bonesetter, Precious Auntie knows where to find more remains, but she will not divulge their location for fear of being haunted by the ancestors to whom those remains belonged. Meanwhile, Chang steals bones from Precious Auntie and sells them. LuLing is sent

Luling's childhood village is known for being the site of the Peking Man discovery. This reconstruction shows the strong resemblance between that early man and modern humans.

PEKING MAN

In 1927, physician and physical anthropologist Davidson Black found a single tooth of what appeared to be human remains at Zhoukoudian, Wade-Giles Chou-k'ou-tien, near the village of Zhoukoudian. From this tooth Black was able to postulate "the existence of distinct form of early man"[9] known as Peking Man. Further excavation revealed other bones: skulls, mandibles (lower jawbones), other facial bones and limb bones. What made this discovery so significant is that so many of the bones were similar to those of modern man. For example, Peking man's cranial capacity averaged between 1,000 to 1,300 cubic centimeters, very close to modern man. There were some differences: Experts believe that Peking man's skull was flat in profile, with very thick skull bones, and that he had a small forehead, a large palate, and a large jaw with no chin. But his teeth closely resembled those of modern man's, and his limb bones were practically identical to those of current humans.[10]

The find was significant because it placed Peking man closer to modern-day humans than other previous remains.

Interestingly, the original bones were being studied and stored at a Peking Union Medical College. But in 1941, when the Japanese were about to invade China, someone tried to smuggle them out of China and into the United States. They never made it, however; all that exists are the plaster casts made of them when they were first discovered.

to Peking for an arranged marriage to Fu Nan, who it turns out, is Chang's son. For his part, Chang hopes to get LuLing to reveal the location of more bones. Precious Auntie is violently opposed to the marriage, but LuLing cannot believe anything bad about her fiancé. The two fight.

In the next chapter, "Ghost," Precious Auntie records the story of her life, while the rest of the Liu clan prepares for LuLing's wedding. Realizing that she cannot stop this marriage, Precious Auntie kills herself and sends a note to the Changs declaring that her ghost will haunt them forever if the marriage goes through. Meanwhile, LuLing reads Precious Auntie's complete story and discovers that Precious Auntie is her real mother. Mother no longer wants to keep LuLing, and though GaoLing treats her kindly, no one else in the Liu clan does. LuLing is sent to an orphanage.

American missionaries run the orphanage, which shares space with the scientists who are analyzing the bones of Peking Man. Precious Auntie had taught LuLing to read and write, so she passes time in the orphanage teaching others. Eventually, she receives a letter from GaoLing and learns that she married Chang Fu Nan and is very unhappy because the man is an opium addict, and she is always looking for money to support his habit. LuLing meets one of the visiting scientists, Kai Jing and they fall in love.

The couple wants to get married, but this is the time when the Japanese are gearing up to invade Peking. The day after the first attack, GaoLing appears at the orphanage and decides she will stay because things have become so strained between her and her husband. LuLing and Kai Jing marry, but almost immediately he is drafted into the Communist army. Eventually, he is murdered by the Japanese. This leaves LuLing bereft, and the only way she is able to carry on is by working at the orphanage.

Once the United States joins the war against Japan, the orphanage is no longer safe, and LuLing and GaoLing make a harrowing escape to Peking. There, they find former students of the orphanage and wait out the war by running an ink shop. The war ends in 1945, and one of the Americans who ran the orphanage, Miss Grutoff, is released from a POW camp, quite ill. GaoLing is selected to accompany her to the United States while LuLing goes to Hong Kong. She waits to hear from GaoLing, who writes to say that Miss Grutoff has died and that life in the States is hard and expensive, but that she is trying to sponsor LuLing. LuLing wants to go back to Peking but cannot afford the train fare, so she begins working as maid. Eventually, GaoLing writes that she is going to remarry, become an American citizen, and sponsor LuLing's entry into the United States. This section of the book ends with LuLing finding the money for passage by selling the oracle bone Precious Auntie gave her. Viewed metaphorically, the bone is the very essence of LuLing and her heritage. By selling it, she is giving up her past and moving not only to a new continent, but a new way of existence.

Part Three returns us to the present. Ruth is living with her mother full-time: "She was her mother's child and the mother to the child her mother had become."[11] This gives her time to reflect on her relationship with Art. She tells her friend Wendy that she doesn't feel lonelier without Art, but more like herself.[12] Gradually, Art and his daughters come to realize they miss her and begin visiting her at her mother's. Meanwhile, Mr. Tang has finished translating LuLing's papers and pays a visit, getting LuLing to recall more of her memories. Ruth lets Art read the translation of LuLing's memoirs, and they talk about their own relationship. Art lets Ruth know that he does love and value her, but he could not see this until she moved out. He also says he has been thinking about the future, about the fact that her mother will regress more and more and will need professional, full-time care that Ruth, who has her own life, cannot give. He has done research and has found the best assisted-living facility for LuLing. He has also devised an elaborate ruse to get LuLing to move, pretending that LuLing must move for a few months due to a radon leak in her apartment and that her relocation will be paid for by the state of California. In fact, Art tells Ruth that he wants to pay for the first three months. The family gathers at GaoLing's to celebrate her birthday, and Ruth speaks with GaoLing alone in the kitchen. Ruth lets her know that she is aware that Precious Auntie is LuLing's mother, and she also knows what happened in China between the two women.

As the book closes, we are brought full circle. Another August has come, but this time Ruth does not lose her voice and feels free of the weight of her mother's superstitions. LuLing herself appears to be happier, lighter. Ruth, who has always been a ghostwriter, decides she will write under her own name, a story that is "for her grandmother, for herself, for the little girl who became her mother."[13]

Structure

The novel is divided into three parts. Part One takes place in San Francisco and focuses on Ruth, a middle-aged ghostwriter living with her boyfriend and his children. Ruth seems to be going through an identity crisis: her relationship with her boyfriend is lacking; and with her mother, "a Chinese immigrant who has always been a figure of unwelcome dominance,"[14] Ruth maintains a stiff and uneasy distance. LuLing has been exhibiting signs of confusion, and Ruth, in searching for the reason, takes her to the doctor, who diagnoses dementia. Ruth ponders the odd answers her mother gives the doctor, realizing that it is not only the dementia but also that her mother is actually revealing secrets from her past. Ruth also realizes that she may lose her mother and along with her, the family's history.

Part Two is LuLing's first-person narrative, a manuscript written in Chinese calligraphy before she began to lose her memory. Though LuLing had given Ruth a copy to read through, the manuscript that Ruth discovers is different, and she resolves to get it translated. This manuscript is Tan's literary device to bridge the present and the past. Through Mr. Tang, the translator, Ruth gains access to her mother's world,

The Bonesetter's Daughter: The Opera

Tan's gift for writing extends not to just to novels and exposition, but to opera libretto as well. Composer Stewart Wallace asked her to write down some ideas for an early scene in his opera of *The Bonesetter's Daughter* when another writer withdrew from the project. Tan wasn't sure how to do it but knew from writing the script for the novel's movie version that the performers and the medium would be more critical than the actual words in bringing the stage version to life.

According to a review in *SFGate*, anyone familiar with the book would see that the opera remains true to the book's themes, but diverges from it as well.[15] The cast is large and features Chinese and Western singers and some fabulous costumes. To underscore the theme of mother-daughter relationships that figure significantly in this novel, one singer, Zheng Cao, is cast in the roles of both Ruth and LuLing.

where she is astonished to learn her mother's history: her first marriage, widowhood, and escape from an orphanage and subsequent emigration to the United States, where she marries Edwin Young. We see Ruth's childhood from LuLing's point of view: raising Ruth alone, a child who does not obey and resents her mother's foreignness.

In Part Three, the focus returns to Ruth, as she decides how to process the information from her mother' story. This leads her to realize she must make major changes in her life, culminating in her finding her own voice.

Themes

Bones

In this novel, bones are a metaphor for healing. In LuLing's narrative, they literally provide a cure: Bonesetter Gu, Ruth's great grandfather, ground bones into healing powder and used the powder to "bind shattered limbs and splayed joints of quarrymen."[16] Much later, the discovery of Peking Man draws scientists to Dragon Bone Hill, the very place where LuLing has grown up. One of those scientists is Pan Kai Jing, whom LuLing marries. For decades, villagers believed that the bones belonged to dragons and this gave them magical powers. Precious Auntie gives LuLing an oracle bone which allegedly allows the owner to ask questions of gods, but it also serves as a constant connection from LuLing to Precious Auntie.

first-person narrative

A story that is told from the point of view of one of the characters. He or she may offer opinions about the action and characters.

More symbolically, bones signify ancestry and Chinese heritage, especially during the time of civil war. Excavation of bones, like the unearthing of secrets and old loves, makes for a satisfying conclusion to the novel.[17] Ruth renews her romance with Art, and provides LuLing with a suitor in Mr. Tang. Affection and forgiveness prevail in the epilogue as LuLing is able to let go of her sorrows and remember that she has, in fact, been loved.

Families

The Bonesetter's Daughter tells the story of three generations of women, mother to daughter to granddaughter. Tan exposes "the pain and conflict in these relationships that cause the women to struggle with each other, as well as the love and loyalty that keeps them together."[18] The way "family" is defined varies throughout this novel. First, LuLing is adopted by Mother to avoid any scandal about Precious Auntie being pregnant before marriage. Long after LuLing and GaoLing settle in the United States and marry two brothers, they keep up the myth of sisterhood, ostensibly so as not to upset their husbands, but also because they themselves have become so accustomed to thinking this way. Ironically, is only LuLing's declining memory that seems to have stirred up the need to get the past "right."

Ruth's status with Art and his daughters represents another kind of family, in a way repeating the same "outsider" status LuLing experienced once her mother committed suicide. Once Ruth becomes more resolved about herself—which happens when she embraces her past— she can accept Art's marriage offer.

Though LuLing and GaoLing are technically cousins, they behave the way the sisters do: they stick up for each other, bicker with each other, and despite catty comments, do lend each other a hand. Family ties are the underpinnings for the whole story; "through strings of relationships, a heritage is built."[19] When Ruth is ready to learn about her past, she becomes stronger in relation to her mother, her boyfriend, and herself.

Superstitions

People in prerevolutionary China relied heavily on superstition to help them make everyday decisions. Fortune-telling was one such superstition. Both smitten with Precious Auntie, Chang and Baby Uncle each go to a different fortune-teller to find out if their birth dates combine favorably with Precious Auntie. Chang's fortune-teller tells him that because he was born in a Snake year and she was born in a Rooster year, the match will be excellent. Baby Uncle's fortune-teller predicts nothing but disaster. But he pays his fortune-teller more "not as a tip but to make her think harder," and she does, finding a different, more positive interpretation of her first reading. To ensure the success of the marriage, "the fortune-teller sold Baby Uncle a Hundred Different Things charm that covered bad dates, bad spirits, bad luck and hair loss."[20]

Ghosts are another staple of traditional Chinese culture, and they are often harbingers of bad luck. If a ghost is peaceful and happy, it will not stay behind to haunt the dead. One must be sure to give ghosts the dead proper and respectful treatment or risk incurring their wrath, a theme often found in Tan's novels. In *The Bonesetter's Daughter*, the ghosts seem particularly strong in the parts of the novel that take place in China. They inhabit people's dreams and show up when they are least expected. After Precious Auntie commits suicide, Mother has the cook throw the body in the ravine near their house. Precious Auntie's ghost seeks revenge on the family, causing the family ink shop to burn down.

The characters of Chang and Baby Uncle each go to fortune-tellers to determine if they are a good match with Precious Auntie. Today, many people still visit these fortune-tellers, like the one seen here.

People celebrate Chinese New Year. Chinese cultural beliefs hold that the start of a new year sets the tone for the entire year to come.

CHINESE SUPERSTITION?

How many of the superstitions in Amy Tan's writing are products of the author's memory or are deeply rooted in Chinese culture? Here are some explanations:

The Chinese believe that the start of the New Year is an opportunity for a new beginning, and that what happens on that first day of the New Year sets the tone for the rest of the year. In order to ensure a successful year, any number of customs may be followed: "The giving of red envelopes or 'ang pao' to children; getting a hair-cut but without washing the hair so that good luck is not washed away; paying all debts and avoid lending money; cleaning the entire house the day before new year so as not to sweep good fortune away; avoiding the use of sharp, pointy objects as they may cut off fortune; and of course buying lucky charms and feasting on prosperity."[21]

Each year has special colors associated with it; for example, the colors of 2013 (the year of the Water Snake) were gold, silver, yellow, beige, and brown.

There are five lucky fruits: Pomelo, pineapple, apple, banana, orange; plus a bunch of Chinese celery and spring onion (with roots). Each of these have special significance; for example, celery signifies hard work and the spring onion intelligence.

The kitchen god is perhaps a relative of the stove god (Zao-wang), which was a way that ancient Chinese symbolized the "sacredness of the hearth fire." "Bronze Age Chinese dwellings all had a central opening for smoke called 'the center of the house.'" Underneath it was ground that was sacred to the home's guardian god. This was where food was made and the family ate their meals, had meetings, and worshiped. "Originally, the god represented the mystery of fire, guardianship of the house ground, and the family's ideals and traditions."[22]

Once in the United States, the superstitions do not seem as potent, especially for GaoLing, who takes to Western culture much more readily than LuLing. Still, LuLing clings to the idea that her family has been cursed and passes these thoughts on to Ruth. It's only in her demented state that she reconsiders a lifetime of traditional superstitions. In the epilogue, she calls Ruth asking for forgiveness—"I'm worried that I did terrible things to you when you were a child, that I hurt you very much. But I can't remember what I did . . . I just wanted to say that I hope you can forget just as I've forgotten. I hope you can forgive me, because if I hurt you, I'm sorry."[23]

Amy Tan Today

Amy Tan has written nine works of fiction thus far in her career. Her most recent novel, *Valley of Amazement*, was published in 2013, eight years after her previous novel, *Saving Fish from Drowning*. In an interview with National Public Radio, Tan reveals that she was two hundred pages into writing when she went to an exhibition about Shanghai in the 1920s. Thinking it would help her with her new novel, she bought a book at the show entitled *The Ten Beauties in Shanghai, 1911*, which examined the life of the Shanghai courtesan in the early 1900s. (A courtesan is a woman who is paid to have sex with wealthy or important men.) These courtesans, Tan discovered, "were not just pretty flowers waiting for male patrons to visit with gifts and money. They were responsible for popularizing Western culture in the city, and enhanced its reputation as an international destination."[1]

The photos in this book struck Tan as strangely familiar. Half of the women pictured were "dressed in snug silk jackets with high, fur-lined collars and three-quarter-length sleeves that displayed long, white sleeves underneath. Several of the women were wearing tight headbands embroidered with pearls. The shape of the headbands brought the wearer's forehead to a comely V shape, and the tension pulled the eye upward, into the much-desired Phoenix eye shape. The wardrobe and the look were all part of the courtesan's official ensemble."[2]

Tan attends an awards ceremony in 2015.

Tan recalled a picture of her grandmother dressed in exactly the same way. And that got her thinking: Was her maternal grandmother ever a courtesan? If so, why? According to family history, her grandmother married late, had two children, and was widowed when her husband died in the 1918 influenza pandemic. "She went to live with her brother, who, Tan says, was cheap and provided her and the children with only the barest of necessities."[3] Of course, suggesting this to anyone in her family would be upsetting, but it was enough for Amy Tan to scrap her original two hundred pages and begin work on what would become *The Valley of Amazement*, a story about a woman from a good family — like her grandmother — who must make a life for herself after suddenly finding herself in need of support.

Beyond Writing

Though writing is her main pursuit, Ms. Tan has many others. A visit to her website quickly confirms this. There, she has a Twitter feed, links to her Facebook page (74,170 likes and counting) and Instagram. In an October 2014 interview with the *Philippine Star*, the sixty-three year-old Tan allowed that it took a little time for her to get the hang of what to do with her Instagram feed:

> I see people who post, and it's mostly about "My book is on sale!" And I'd do that. When I started doing more of it, it was because the publisher thought it would be helpful. It took me a while to figure out what to post about. So I thought I'll just post about what I found interesting for the day, and often it has to do with travel, attitudes, sometimes politics. I've posted my dog sniffing around with my luggage. For a number of hours while I was at the airport, it was "You know you're going

> to Asia when you can get noodles at the airport lounge," or "You know that when you see people criticizing the food and talking about how they can make it cheaper, you know you're going to Asia." I'll put that in, because it's humorous.[4]

Tan is an avid traveler, and she supports a variety of charities including Lyme4Kids, an organization devoted to preventing Lyme disease, a debilitating bacterial disease transmitted by the bite of a deer tick. (Tan herself has suffered from the disease for many years.) In a 2015 post on her Facebook page, Tan mentions that she and her husband contribute to charities that address a wide range of causes including the elderly, children, the ill, the Asian community, and the environment.

In addition to appearing as an extra in the movie version of *The Joy Luck Club*, Tan's voice and likeness appeared on the "Insane Poppy Clown" episode of *The Simpsons* in 2000. When interviewed about this appearance by staff writers for *Crew* magazine, Ms. Tan said:

> [Creator] Matt Groening asked if I would do it, and he also volunteered to direct me . . . So there I was in a studio, connected to Matt, who was directing me. I was saying to Lisa Simpson, after she had complimented me on my tender mother-daughter stories . . . I'm berating her for describing erroneously what my book is about. "That's not what I said! That's not what the book is about! Sit down, I'm ashamed for the both of us." Matt went through twenty iterations of that. "Sound meaner, really let her have it." I was trying to get to the point of fomenting, full of madness, berating some poor little girl who would have psychiatric problems the rest of her life! What we ended up with was probably the first take,

which was fairly mild. I sound nasty, but not nearly as much as in the takes Matt cajoled out of me.[5]

Tan is a bit of a public media darling: She has appeared on NPR's *Morning Edition*, *All Things Considered*, *Fresh Air*, and most recently *Wait, Wait Don't Tell Me*. True to the latter show's irreverent style, Ms. Tan was asked (because of her last name) to determine whether anecdotes about tanning and the tanning industry were true or false.[6] Though not her area

Tan attends a charity event with husband, Lou (left), and actor/author Steve Martin.

of expertise, she played along and came through with flying colors.

Amy Tan is also a rock star. Well, sort of. She is part of a group called the Rock Bottom Remainders. Started by fellow writer and author escort Kathi Kamen Goldmark, the group is named for the booksellers' term for books that stay on the shelves so long they must be dumped at a discount. "Composed of a shifting cast of literary luminaries that include Stephen King, Amy Tan, Scott Turow and Dave Barry, the Remainders have come together once a year or so since 1992 to play."[7]

Tan has been with the group for twenty-two years, and though she knows how to play classical piano, she is not the keyboardist. Rather, she walks around in a "ridiculous costume and I sing a ridiculous song. I have a whip, and at the end of my song, "These Boots Are Made for Walking," all the boys turn around, bend over and I whip them! And people go crazy because I'm whipping Stephen King!"[8] To describe their experiences, the band did what they do best: They wrote a book called *Hard Listening*. It's an e-book, available for tablets and e-readers and brings together photos, essays, video, quizzes, and some rock-and-roll advice from quasi-musicians, what reviewer Camila Domonoske calls "less e-book than e-scrapbook, a curated collection of artifacts from a group of friends."[9]

In 2008, Amy Tan was invited to give a TED talk on creativity. TED stands for Technology, Entertainment and Design. It is a nonprofit organization dedicated to spreading ideas through formal talks of eighteen minutes or fewer. Tan's talk began with a discussion of where creativity might come from: Is it something physical, like an abnormal chromosome or brain wiring? Is it a function of an identity crisis; that is, wondering who you are and why you possess the particular

Tan sings with her band, the Rock Bottom Remainders, at a benefit. Other members of the band have included writers Stephen King, Scott Turow, and Dave Barry.

characteristics that you do? Could creativity be linked to trauma and childhood development?

Tan explains that she believes her childhood trauma changed her way of looking at the world and fostered creativity. Tan says that her trauma was the death of her brother and father six months apart. But it was also her mother's reaction to it. Her mother did not believe it was random bad luck; she believed that "there was a reason for everything. And one of the reasons, she thought, was that her mother, who had died when she was very young, was angry at her."[10] Tan says being exposed to this kind of rationalization and trauma so young in life causes one to think deeply about everything; first and foremost because you don't know what may be coming next. This led Tan to ask bigger questions that she still has today: Why do things happen, and how do things happen? And the question her mother had: How do I make things happen? From this sort of questioning Tan believes true creativity arises, out of some sort of necessity or survival instinct. Knowing that the questions are large and do not necessarily have an answer is to discover something new, to stimulate one's imagination, and to create.

Author's Note: On the first page of her website (www.amytanauthor.com), Ms. Tan notes that she created the site by herself and that the autobiography it contains is the "the only one that is 100% correct." Though every effort has been made in the preceding pages to be 100 percent correct, the author humbly states she could hardly know as much about Ms. Tan as Ms. Tan knows about herself. She hopes that anyone reading this book will be encouraged to take their own journey to learn about Amy Tan, her writing, and her life.

Chronology

1952– Amy Tan is born in Oakland, California, to John and Daisy Tan.

1955–1967– Lives in various locations in Northern California.

1967– Tan's brother Peter dies from a brain tumor.

1968– Tan's father, John, also dies of a brain tumor in February, six months after Peter. In August, Daisy Tan decides to move Amy and her brother, John, to the Netherlands. In September, the family travels from Holland, to southern Germany, and finally to Montreux, Switzerland, where Daisy enrolls Amy and John in a private school.

1969– Tan graduates from high school a year early and returns to the United States.

1970–1972– Attends Linfield College in McMinnville, Oregon, on an American Baptist scholarship. Starts college as a premed student. Meets Lou DeMattei, an Italian American law student, who will become her husband. Transfers from Linfield to San Jose City College (California) to be near DeMattei and switches from premed to a double major in linguistics and English.

1973–1974– Transfers to San Jose State, graduates with a BA in English and begins graduate work in linguistics at the University of California, Santa Cruz. Enrolls in postdoctoral program at UC Berkeley and supports herself by working at the Round Table Restaurant in San Jose.

1976– Abandons postgraduate work and marries DeMattei. The couple move to San Francisco.

1980– Tan directs MORE, a program in San Francisco for the developmentally handicapped.

1983– Begins freelance work, writing technical reports for clients such as Apple, AT&T, and IBM.

1987– Enrolls in Squaw Valley Community of Writers Workshop run by published authors. Tan is noticed by writer Molly Giles, who encourages her to continue writing. Tan finds literary agent Sandra Dijkstra. In October, Tan and her mother visit the People's Republic of China. Tan meets her half sisters and finds a connection. Meanwhile Dijkstra informs Tan that she has offers for her stories.

1988– Tan stops freelancing and becomes a full-time fiction writer.

1989– *The Joy Luck Club* is published and endorsed by the well-known authors Louise Erdrich, Alice Hoffman, and Alice Walker.

1991– Her second novel, *The Kitchen God's Wife*, is published to high acclaim. Helps her half sister Jindo and Jindo's daughter and husband relocate from China to Wisconsin.

1992– Tan tries her hand at children's writing, collaborating with illustrator Gretchen Shields on *The Moon Lady*. Joins the band Rock Bottom Remainders and sings at the annual American Booksellers Association meeting in Anaheim.

1993– Despite initial reluctance, Tan allows filming of *The Joy Luck Club*. In August, the Yale-China Association begins a stage version of *The Joy Luck Club* to be performed in Mandarin.

1994– Teams with Gretchen Shields for a second book: *The Chinese Siamese Cat*. In 2001, this book became the basis of the PBS series, *Sagwa, the Chinese Siamese Cat*.

1995– *The Hundred Secret Senses* is published with an initial press run of 550,000 copies. Daisy Tan is diagnosed with Alzheimer's disease.

1999– Daisy Tan dies on November 22 at the age of eighty-three.

2001– *The Bonesetter's Daughter* is published.

2003– Receives a Writers for Writers award, an honorary degree from Simmons College in Boston, and joins other authors in protesting US involvement in Iraq.

2009– Is honored at San Francisco Book Festival.

2013– Coauthors *Hard Listening*, an interactive e-book about her participation in the Rock Bottom Remainders. Releases *Valley of Amazement*.

2015– According to Tan's official website, "The Formerly Defunct Rock Bottom Remainders resurrected themselves at the Miami Book Fair."

Chapter Notes

Chapter 1. Coming to Gold Mountain

1. Amy Tan, "The Best Stories," *The Opposite of Fate: A Book of Musings* (New York: G.P. Putnam's Sons, 2003), p. 334.
2. Ibid., p. 335.
3. John Kuo Wei Tchen in "The Joy Luck Club by Amy Tan," *The Big Read*, October 21, 2015, www.neabigread.org/books/joyluckclub/media/transcript/.
4. Russell Freedman, *Angel Island Gateway to Gold Mountain* (Boston: Clarion Books, 2014), p. 41.
5. John Kuo Wei Tchen.
6. Norma Libman, "Born to Write," *Chicago Tribune* (1963-Current file): 1, July 7, 1991, *ProQuest*, Web, accessed January 1, 2016.
7. Amy Tan in Elaine Woo, "Striking Cultural Sparks Once Pained by Her Heritage, Amy Tan has Tapped It for a Piercing First Novel," *Los Angeles Times* (pre-1997 Fulltext): 1, March 12, 1989, *ProQuest*, Web, accessed November 23, 2015.
8. "Amy Tan," *Newsmakers* (Detroit: Gale, 1998), *Biography in Context*, Web, accessed October 20, 2015.
9. Tan, "The Best Stories," p. 21.
10. Ibid., p. 17
11. Ibid., p. 22.
12. Thomas A. Greenfield, "Route 66," *Daily Life through History*, ABC-CLIO, Web, accessed December 9, 2015.
13. Amy Tan, *The Opposite of Fate* (New York Putnam & Sons, 2003), p. 17.
14. Ibid., p. 30.
15. Matthew James Vechinski, "Staging the Reception of American Ethnic Authors in Women's Popular Magazines:

Encountering Amy Tan's *The Joy Luck Club* Stories in *Seventeen* and *Ladies' Home Journal*," *Reception: Texts, Readers, Audiences, History* 7.1 (2015): 45–63, *Project MUSE*, accessed November 7, 2015, muse.jhu.edu/.

16. Ibid.
17. Ibid.
18. E.D. Huntley, *Amy Tan: A Critical Companion* (Westport, CT: Greenwood Press, 1998), p. 8.

Chapter 2. Major Themes

1. Gayle Feldman, "The Making of Amy Tan's The Joy Luck Club: Chinese magic, American blessings and a publishing fairy tale," *Publisher's Weekly*, July 7, 1989, www.publishersweekly.com/pw/by-topic/authors/profiles/article/58657-the-making-of-the-joy-luck-club.html.
2. Amy Tan, "Required Reading and Other Dangerous Subjects," *The Opposite of Fate: A Book of Musings* (New York: G.P. Putnam's Sons, 2003), p. 305.
3. E.D. Huntley, *Amy Tan: A Critical Companion* (Westport, CT: Greenwood Press, 1998), p. 39.
4. Ibid., p. 32.
5. Linda Ching Sledge, "Maxine Kingston's China Men: The Family Historian as Epic Poet," *MELUS* 7.4 (1980): pp. 3–22, Web, accessed November 17, 2015.
6. Huntley, p. 32.
7. Elaine Woo, "Striking Cultural Sparks Once Pained by Her Heritage, Amy Tan Has Tapped It for a Piercing First Novel," *Los Angeles Times (pre-1997 Fulltext)*: 1, March 12, 1989, *ProQuest*, Web, accessed November 23, 2015.
8. Ibid.
9. Huntley, p. 92

Chapter 3. *The Joy Luck Club*

1. Mary Ellen Snodgrass, *Amy Tan: A Literary Companion* (Jefferson, NC: McFarland & Co., 2004), p. 17.
2. "Amy Tan Biography—Academy of Achievement," Academy of Achievement, June 28, 1996, www.achievement.org/autodoc/page/tan0int-5.
3. E.D. Huntley, *Amy Tan: A Critical Companion* (Westport, CT: Greenwood Press, 1998), p. 43.
4. Matthew James Vechinski, "Staging the Reception of American Ethnic Authors in Women's Popular Magazines: Encountering Amy Tan's *The Joy Luck Club* Stories in *Seventeen* and *Ladies' Home Journal*," *Reception: Texts, Readers, Audiences, History*, 7.1 (2015): pp. 45–63, *Project MUSE*, November 7, 2015, muse.jhu.edu/.
5. Amy Tan, *The Joy Luck Club* (New York: Putnam's, 1989), p. 17.
6. Camille-Yvette Welsh, "Amy Tan: A Look at the Critical Reception," Evans pp. 19–32 in Tara Fickle, "American Rules and Chinese Faces: The Games of Amy Tan's The Joy Luck Club," MELUS: Multi-Ethnic Literature of the U.S. 39.3 (2014): pp. 68–88, Project MUSE, Web, Accessed November 11, 2015. [Robert C. Evans, ed., *The Joy Luck Club* by Amy Tan (Pasadena: Salem, 2010).]
7. Ibid.
8. Sau-ling Cynthia Wong, "'Sugar sisterhood': Situating the Amy Tan Phenomenon," in Harold Bloom, ed., *Bloom's Modern Critical Views – Amy Tan* (New York: Chelsea House Publishers, 2009), pp. 55–56.
9. Tara Fickle, "American Rules and Chinese Faces: The Games of Amy Tan's The Joy Luck Club," MELUS: Multi-

Ethnic Literature of the U.S. 39.3 (2014): pp. 68–88, Project MUSE, Web, accessed November 11, 2015.

10. Tan, *The Joy Luck Club*, p. 83.
11. Ibid., p. 130.
12. Ibid., p. 142.
13. Ibid., p. 254.
14. Ibid., p. 208.
15. Ibid., p. 215.
16. Ibid., p. 239.
17. Ibid., p. 240.
18. Ibid., p. 249.
19. Ibid., p. 250.
20. Ibid., p. 253.
21. Ibid., p. 256.
22. Ibid., p. 266.
23. Ibid., p. 281.
24. Ibid., p. 288.
25. Snodgrass, *Amy Tan: A Literary Companion*, p. 16.
26. Amy Tan, *The Opposite of Fate* (New York Putnam & Sons, 2003), p. 303.
27. Huntley, p. 39.
28. Tan, *The Joy Luck Club*, p. 254.
29. M. Anwar Deeb Gehan, "Between Two Cultures-Finding Meaning in Amy Tan's use of Superstitions," *European Journal of English Language and Literature* 3, no. 3 (July 2015): pp. 76–108.
30. Tan, *The Opposite of Fate*, p. 301.
31. Tan, *The Joy Luck Club*, p. 24.
32. *A Study Guide for Amy Tan's* The Joy Luck Club (Detroit, MI: Gale Research), p. 223.
33. Tan, *The Joy Luck Club*, p. 252.
34. Huntley, p. 58.

35. Tan, *The Joy Luck Club*, p. 28.
36. Huntley, p. 58.
37. Amy Tan in David Armstrong, "Two Worlds, Two Writers for Tan Film Joy Luck Club Movie Matches Author's Vision," *San Francisco Examiner*, Aug 22, 1993, articles.sun-sentinel.com/1993-08-22/entertainment/9308200942_1_movie-ron-bass-wayne-wang.
38. Ibid.
39. "Study Guide for Tan's 'The Joy Luck Club,'" location p. 223.
40. Tan, *The Joy Luck Club*, p. 73.

Chapter 4. *The Kitchen God's Wife*

1. E.D. Huntley, *Amy Tan: A Critical Companion* (Westport, CT: Greenwood Press, 1998), p. 80.
2. Ibid., p. 83.
3. "Sino-Japanese War," Britannica School, *Encyclopædia Britannica*, November 14, 2015, library.eb.com/levels/rcfcrencecenter/article/67946.
4. Amy Tan, *The Kitchen God's Wife* (New York: Vintage, 1993), p. 11.
5. Ibid., p. 115.
6. Ibid., p. 82.
7. Tan, *The Kitchen God's Wife*, p. 54.
8. Ibid.
9. Ibid., p. 55.
10. Mary Ellen Snodgrass, *Amy Tan: A Literary Companion* (Jefferson, NC: McFarland & Co., 2004), p. 95.
11. Tan, *The Kitchen God's Wife*, p. 62.
12. Ibid., p. 68.
13. Ibid., p. 69.
14. Ibid., p. 71.

15. Huntley, p. 87.
16. Tan, *The Kitchen God's Wife*, p. 156.
17. Ibid., p. 152.
18. Ibid., p. 171.
19. Ibid., p. 191.
20. "Sino-Japanese War of 1937–1945," *World History: The Modern Era*, ABC-CLIO, 2015, Web, accessed November 14, 2015.
21. Huntley, p. 82.
22. Elizabeth Thomason, ed., "Amy Tan," *Novels for Students*, vol. 13 (Detroit: Gale, 2002), p. 106.
23. Huntley, p. 105–106.
24. Ibid.
25. Tan, *The Kitchen God's Wife*, p. 29.
26. Ibid., p. 82.
27. Ibid., p. 91.
28. Charles Benn, "Foodstuffs in China: Tang Dynasty," *Daily Life through History*, ABC-CLIO, 2015, Web, accessed December 10, 2015.
29. Ibid.
30. Ibid.
31. Stephanie Fogel, "dim sum," *Daily Life through History*, ABC-CLIO, 2015, December 10, 2015.
32. Ibid.
33. Tan, *The Kitchen God's Wife*, p. 235.
34. Ibid.
35. Ibid., p. 62.
36. Ibid., p. 89.
37. Ibid.
38. Norman Libman, "Born to write, Amy Tan pursues a quest to make sense of the world," *Chicago Tribune*

(Pre-1997 Fulltext), July 7, 1991, search.proquest.com/docview/283192973?accountid=13567.

39. Amy Tan Biography—Academy of Achievement," Academy of Achievement, June 28, 1996, www.achievement.org/autodoc/page/tan0int-5.
40. Tan, *The Kitchen God's Wife*, p. 123.
41. Ibid., p. 239.
42. Ibid., p. 242.
43. Ibid., p. 192.
44. Ibid., p. 236.
45. Ibid., p. 62.
46. Ibid., p. 69.

Chapter 5. *The Bonesetter's Daughter*

1. Sara Constantakis, ed., "Overview: *The Bonesetter's Daughter*," *Novels for Students*, vol. 31 (Detroit: Gale, 2010), *Literature Resource Center*, Web, accessed December 7, 2015.
2. Amy Tan, *The Bonesetter's Daughter* (New York: Ballantine, 2002), p. 5.
3. Ibid., p. 46.
4. Ibid., p. 146.
5. Ibid., p. 149.
6. Ibid., p. 151.
7. Ibid., p. 153.
8. Ibid., p. 182.
9. Davidson Black, "Peking Man," Britannica School, *Encyclopædia Britannica*, 2015. Web, accessed December 14, 2015.
10. Ibid.
11. Tan, *The Bonesetter's Daughter*, p. 315.
12. Ibid., p. 317.

13. Ibid., p. 368.
14. Nancy Dziedzic, "Overview of The Bonesetter's Daughter," *Gale Literary Overviews* (Detroit: Gale, 2012), Literature Resource Center, Web, December 7, 2015.
15. Steven Winn, "Amy Tan's Opera: 'The Bonesetter's Daughter,'" August 24, 2008, *SFGate*, www.sfgate.com/entertainment/article/Amy-Tan-s-opera-The-Bonesetter-s-Daughter-3271943.php.
16. Mary Ellen Snodgrass, *Amy Tan: A Literary Companion* (Jefferson, NC: McFarland & Co., 2004), p. 43.
17. Ibid.
18. Sara Constantakis, ed., "The Bonesetter's Daughter," *Novels for Students*, vol. 31 (Detroit: Gale, 2010), pp. 1–25, *Gale Virtual Reference Library*, Web, December 15, 2015.
19. Ibid.
20. Tan, *The Bonesetter's Daughter*, p. 177.
21. "Of lucky charms and delicious superstitions," *Manila Times* [Manila, Philippines] February 7, 2013, *World History in Context*, Web.
22. Kathryn Allen Abuzzi, "Home," *Encyclopedia of Religion*, 2nd ed., vol. 6 (Detroit: Macmillan Reference USA, 2005), pp. 4104–4107, *World History in Context*, Web, accessed December 17, 2015.
23. Tan, *The Bonesetter's Daughter*, p. 367.

Chapter 6. Amy Tan Today

1. Karen Grigsby Bates, "Amy Tan Weaves Family Mystery into 'Valley of Amazement,'" *Code Switch*, November 4, 2013, transcript, www.npr.org/templates/transcript/transcript.php?storyId=242926707.

2. Karen Grigsby Bates, "Amy Tan Weaves Family Mystery into 'Valley of Amazement,'" *Code Switch*, November 4, 2013, www.npr.org/sections/codeswitch/2013/11/04/242926707/amy-tan-weaves-family-mystery-into-valley-of-amazement.
3. Ibid.
4. Chonx Tibajia, "Amy Tan on joy, luck and life of writing," *The Philippine Star*, October 25, 2014, www.philstar.com/modern-living/2014/10/25/1383994/amy-tan-joy-luck-and-life-writing.
5. "Amy Tan On Writing and Being On 'The Simpsons,'" *Crew*, December 14, 2013, www.crewmagazine.com/article/amy-tan-writes/.
6. "We Quiz Novelist Amy on Tanning Techniques," April 11, 2015, National Public Radio, www.npr.org/2015/04/11/398798389/we-quiz-novelist-amy-tan-on-tanning-techniques.
7. Douglas Martin, "Kathi Kame Goldmark, Writers' catalyst dies at 63," *New York Times*, May 30, 2012, www.nytimes.com/2012/05/30/books/kathi-kamen-goldmark-writers-catalyst-dies-at-63.html?_r=0.
8. Tibajia, "Amy Tan on joy, luck and life of writing."
9. Camila Domonoske, "Digital Scrapbook Collects Rock-star Authors' memories," National Public Radio, June 17, 2013, radio.krcb.org/post/digital-scrapbook-collects-rock-star-authors-memories#stream/0.
10. Amy Tan, "Where does creativity hide?" *TED Talk*, February 2008, 04:13. www.ted.com/talks/amy_tan_on_creativity/transcript?language=en.

Literary Terms

anecdote—A brief story about something that happens to a person.

fable—A story intended to teach a lesson and in which animals take on the characteristics of humans.

first-person narrative—A story that is told from the point of view of one of the characters. He or she may offer opinions about the action and characters.

flashback—A way of relating the present story to something that happened before the story takes place. Dreams and memories are a way of incorporating flashbacks into a story.

imagery— The use of language to create an image, or a picture in the reader's mind, about how something looks, sounds, or feels.

leitmotiv—Recurrence of images, objects, or actions in story or a body of literature. It can also be the repetition of certain words or phrases in a work. One of Tan's leitmotivs is the relationship between mothers and daughters.

metaphor—A word or phrase used to compare one thing to another in order to show a similarity; for example, "She's a broken record, going on and on about the same things."

myth—A story, often involving gods or other superhuman beings, that is told in order to explain a custom, belief, or event.

perspective—Point of view.

symbol—Something that stands for or represents another thing.

Major Works by Amy Tan

Fiction

The Joy Luck Club (novel), 1989
The Kitchen God's Wife (novel), 1991
The Hundred Secret Senses (novel), 1995
The Best American Short Stories, 1999, (guest editor), 1999
The Bonesetter's Daughter (novel), 2001
Saving Fish from Drowning (novel), 2005
The Valley of Amazement (novel), 2013

Nonfiction

The Opposite of Fate: A Book of Musings, 2003

Children's Books

The Moon Lady, 1992
The Chinese Siamese Cat, 1994

Further Reading

Becnel, Kim. *Bloom's How to Write About Amy Tan*. New York: Bloom's Literary Criticism Series, 2010.

Freedman, Russel. *Angel Island: Gateway to Gold Mountain*. New York: Clarion, 2013.

Tam, Holland. *The Counterfeit Family Tree of Vee Crawford-Wong*. New York: Simon & Schuster, 2013.

Uschan, Mike. *Chinese Mythology*. San Diego: Lucent, 2014.

Yang, Gene Luen. *American Born Chinese*. New York: First Second, 2006.

Yee, Paul. *Chinese Fairy Tale Feasts: A Literary Cookbook*. Northampton, MA: Crocodile Books, 2014.

Websites

Amy Tan
amytanauthor.com
The author's own site includes biography, readings, photos, and her blog.

Academy of Achievement – Amy Tan
www.achievement.org/autodoc/page/tan0bio-1
Provides a profile, biography, interview, and photo gallery.

Steven Barclay Agency – Amy Tan
barclayagency.com/site/speaker/amy-tan
Features complete list of titles, videos, and links to Tan-related sites.

Index